An Early History of

Spirit Lake &
The Toutle River Valley

by Leland Jackson

with Trudy Howarth

Printed under Sponsorship of the Castle Rock Exhibit Hall Society

Published in 1995 by Leland Jackson and Trudy Howarth

Permission is granted by the authors to anyone who wishes to use any portion of this book, except for the copyrighted article from *Skamania County Heritage* on page 34.

FIRST EDITION

RED APPLE PUBLISHING
P. O. Box 101
Gig Harbor, WA 98335

Printed by Gorham Printing
Rochester, Washington 98579

ISBN: 1-880222-26-4

Library of Congress Catalog Card Number 95-71891

Cover illustration by Jessie Richardson, Gig Harbor, Washington

Page and cover design by Kathyrn E. Campbell

TOOTLE LAKE OR TOUTLE LAKE?
BUREAU OF TOPOLOGICAL ENGINEERING, 1859

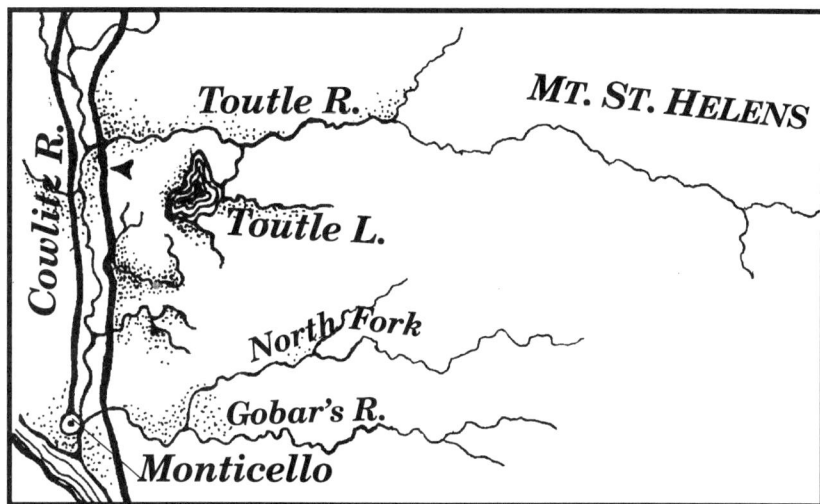

Toutle R.   MT. ST. HELENS

Cowlitz R.

Toutle L.

North Fork

Gobar's R.

Monticello

The above map is probably the first, fairly accurate, surveyed plat of this area. Prior to this survey, the mouth of the Toutle River was commonly known as the Forks of the Cowlitz River. The stream known as Gobar's River was not renamed the Coweeman River until a later date.

Two roads on either side of the Cowlitz River are shown. The old Hudson's Bay Road shown on the east bank was little more than a trail connecting Fort Vancouver with Fort Nisqually on Puget Sound. There were several fairly large streams that had to be forded. The newly surveyed and partially finished Military Road is shown on the west bank. This road being laid out on high ground and ridges had no major streams to cross south of central Lewis County.

Before the early 1860s, flatboats and canoes were the common means of travel through this region, as steamboats were rare and the roads were not yet ready for wheeled vehicles.

Some early maps show a village named Silver Lake on the northwest shore of Toutle Lake.

Note: The arrow points to the location of the "later-to-be" town of Castle Rock.

EARLY NORTHERN COWLITZ COUNTY

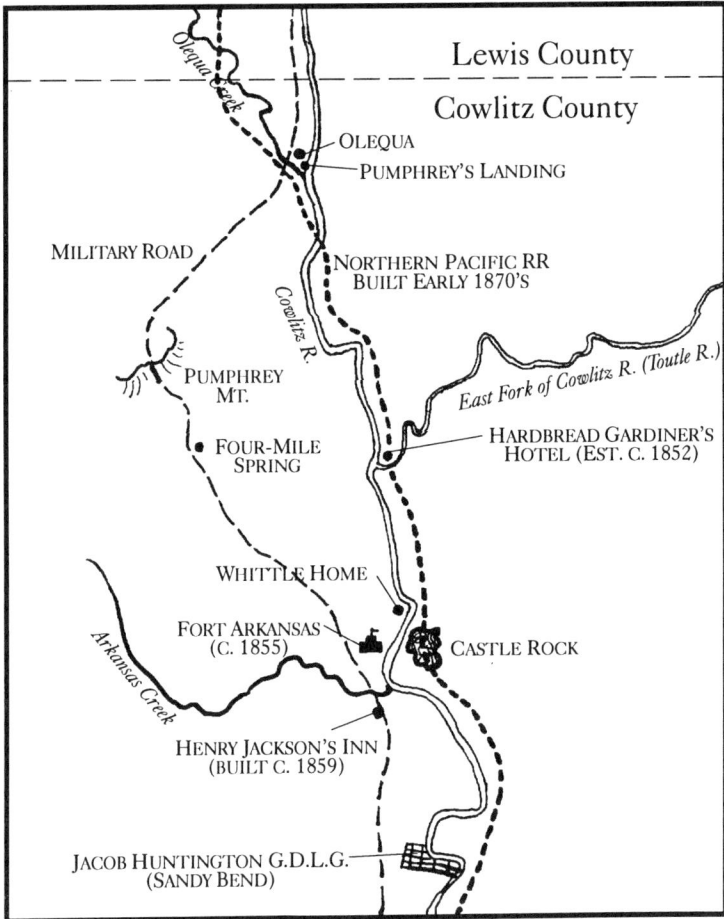

Lewis County

Cowlitz County

Olequa Creek

OLEQUA

PUMPHREY'S LANDING

MILITARY ROAD

NORTHERN PACIFIC RR
BUILT EARLY 1870'S

Cowlitz R.

PUMPHREY
MT.

East Fork of Cowlitz R. (Toutle R.)

FOUR-MILE
SPRING

HARDBREAD GARDINER'S
HOTEL (EST. C. 1852)

WHITTLE HOME

Arkansas Creek

FORT ARKANSAS
(C. 1855)

CASTLE ROCK

HENRY JACKSON'S INN
(BUILT C. 1859)

JACOB HUNTINGTON G.D.L.G.
(SANDY BEND)

Total Area in the Watershed of the Toutle River & Tributaries

335,000 acres, 523 square miles—Art Jones 2-1-93

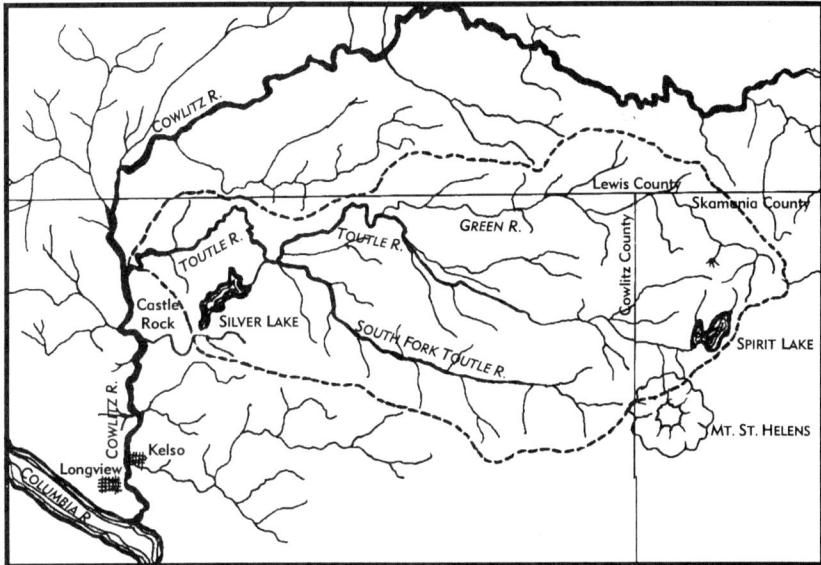

The Toutle River drainage system takes up a large part of the northeast quadrant of Cowlitz County. After emptying into the Cowlitz River, the Toutle River follows an often narrow-winding valley for some 12 miles where it splits into two major branches that terminate on the west and north sides of Mt. St. Helens. A third branch, the Green River, leaves the North Fork some 10 miles farther east and drains the northeast corner of Cowlitz and a small part of Skamania County. It carries no St. Helens water.

This vast area of some 14 or 15 townships was once heavily timbered with fir, cedar and hemlock. There was, however, an exceptional area, a rather narrow ribbon of brushy, lightly timbered, shoreland that encircles Silver Lake (earlier name: Toutle Lake). This land could be converted to pasture and garden space with little labor.

POST CARD

LANGE, WASH.
OCT 20 A.M. 1915

Dear Julia —
Don't
send the Baby's
here — I want them
to have when we
get to town —
write soon,
your sister,
Lillian —

Miss Julia Lange
Castle Rock
Wash.

Mt. St. Helens & Lange History

Most of the following history was collected by my mother, Georgia Lange McCoy, who lived in Castle Rock until about 1948, when she married Peter Pehrsson and moved to Tacoma. She passed away in July of 1986.

The articles from the *Cowlitz County Advocate* are from the columns "From Past *Advocates*" and "Good Old Days."

Grandpa and Grandma Lange histories are from Lillian Lange Thomas, as are most of the early-day photos and some genealogy information from Grandpa Lange's sister Julia.

General mining information is from *St. Helens Mining District, A Condensed History* by R.H. McClure, Jr., of the Forest Service, printed in the *Skamania County Heritage*, which did not list Grandpa Lange's mine.

—Mary McCoy Whitney
Granddaughter of the Langes

Foreword

Some of the hardy folks who moved to the Pacific Northwest in the late 18th Century were motivated by dreams of getting rich. The prospect of adventure brought others. But, it was economic necessity that prompted the westward movement of pioneers who settled the Toutle River Valley and Silver Lake areas. Most came in search of better lives after enduring hardship and misfortune in drought-stricken Midwest states. Some lost family members and personal belongings during treks that took them across the Plains and over the Rocky Mountains to start life anew in territory they had never seen, yet gave them hope.

This book, by Northern Cowlitz County Historian Leland Jackson and staff, compiled with family histories, letters, documents and other material provided by their descendants, tells their stories. Minimal editing was done, other than shortening some accounts in the interest of conserving space and clarification. In instances where histories were furnished by more than one member of the same family, the material was combined to avoid duplication.

While most of the stories relate to settlement of the Toutle and Silver Lake areas, the book includes a fascinating account of early development at Mt. St. Helens and Spirit Lake by Robert C. Lange.

Lange, an immigrant of Austrian and German descent, fought and defeated the U.S. Forest Service to obtain a patent for what became the only successful homestead in the area. He not only mined there but also operated a sawmill that furnished lumber for most buildings that were erected. Some property in the region was still owned by the Lange family when the mountain erupted on May 18, 1980.

In addition to the pioneers who left the Midwest to escape that region's harsh economic conditions were Scandinavians who settled in the area later named Kid Valley, as well as other nearby locations beyond Green Mountain.

Besides relating the experiences of those who homesteaded and raised their families in the Silver Lake and Toutle areas, the book describes how they banded together to build schools and hire teachers to meet the educational needs of their children.

Some farmed for a living, some worked in the shingle industry that was a prominent local industry in that era, and some became loggers or worked at other blue-collar trades. A very few were merchants who provided necessities the settlers couldn't grow or produce themselves.

The common thread running through their stories was the pioneer spirit that enabled them to travel many miles at considerable risk to make better lives for their families.

They shall not be forgotten.

—Bud May, president, Castle Rock Exhibit Hall Society

THE CASTLE ROCK EXHIBIT HALL SOCIETY

The Castle Rock Exhibit Hall Society is a non-profit entity dedicated to preserving the history of the town of Castle Rock and Northern Cowlitz County. This history, in the form of old photographs, logging equipment, implements and other exhibits, is displayed in the Castle Rock Exhibit Hall. The Hall's three galleries are entitled *The River, The Mountain* and *Our Town*.

Contents

PART I—THE LANGE FAMILY

   1   History of the Lange Family
   3   General Mine Information
   5   Lange's Mine
   8   Fire Story
   9   Mine Story
 10   Some Proposals or Projects That Didn't Make It
 13   The Homestead
 13   The Yacolt Fire, 1902
 14   Our First Family Trip
 14   Forest Fire Musings
 15   Mine Story—The German Engineer
 16   Patent Problems
 21   Community
 21   Lillian's Store at the Lake
 21   Gratia Huntington—Castle Rock Pioneer
 22   Building and the Sawmill
 24   Leased Land
 24   Other Developments and Happenings
 25   Phones
 26   Papa Versus You-Know-Who and Other Family Memories
 26   The Decade of the 1920s
 27   1924 and Sasquatch
 27   Enter Harry Truman
 28   The Homestead in My Day
 28   The Store Building
 29   The Depression
 33   Auto-stage to Spirit Lake, Washington
 33   R.C. Lange Rented Boats at Spirit Lake in 1902
 34   The St. Helens Mining District: A Condensed History (copyrighted article)
 38   St. Helens Mines
 39   Portland YMCA Boys' Camp at Spirit Lake

PART II—VERY EARLY HISTORY

 47   The Beginning
 48   James Gardiner
 50   Tower—Settlements along the Toutle River
 53   Poria
 54   The Storm Family
 56   Very Early Silver Lake
 56   The Jacob Tippery Family

61   The Miles Tippery and Will Tippery Families
63   The R.S. Carnine Family
65   Mangs Family Tree Has Gardner Branches
66   Silver Lake Schools
67   Woodard
68   Green River Bridge
69   Francisco Stage
69   Frank G. Barnes and Silver Lake, Washington
71   The Silver Lake Railway and Lumber Company
75   First Settlers of Toutle Area Found River to Be Both Obstacle
      & Source of Livelihood
76   1882 and 1889 Immigrations
77   Rugged Conditions
77   Long Hard Winters
78   Industry Lifesaver
78   Homes Deserted
79   Schools Established
79   Post Office Established
80   Celebrations Marked
81   Napoleon Bonepart Gardner Brought Family to Toutle River Area in 1882
81   Decision Reversed
82   Disaster Strikes
83   Many Destitute
83   Mangs Arrive
87   David Gardner, Civil War Vet, Came to Toutle in 1883
88   The Frank Smith Story
90   Some Settlers of Toutle and Green Mountain
90   Some Settlers of Green River, North of Toutle River
90   Kid Valley
91   Some Settlers of Kid Valley
91   Wm. Henry Chism Had Twelve Children
93   Some Settlers of St. Helens Valley

PART III—THE RAILROAD, MILLS & SHINGLES

 97   The 1880s
 98   John Robin
100   Shingles
102   Cedar Drives on Toutle Required Tough Men

PART IV—THE MT. ST. HELENS AREA

109   Historical Data
113   Afterword

PART I

The Lange Family

History of The Lange Family

by Mary McCoy Whitney

The history of the Lange family is interwoven with that of the Mt. St. Helens and Spirit Lake history. My grandfather, Robert C. Lange, was an interesting, talented visionary with big plans for the Spirit Lake country and many adventures. He was an early-day miner. He had a saw-mill which furnished lumber used in most of the early buildings. He fought the Forest Service to obtain a patent for homestead land, and won. That was the only successful homestead in the area and some of the property was still owned by the Lange family at the time of the eruption. The remainder had been sold over time for vacation cabins. If he had kept a journal, what tales it could tell.

When the mountain was emerging from its period of dormancy in 1980, and every time the TV was turned on then, there was Harry Truman sitting on his front porch spouting off the same independent character I remember from the late 1920s and 1930s. I thought of my grandfather as the true pioneer in the settling of that country, and yet he was barely mentioned in the books that came out after the eruption. So, I would like to add some of what I know of our Lange and Mt. St. Helens history. Some is taken from notes written by my mother, Georgia Lange, who wanted to write a book but was too busy living.

Robert C. Lange was born in 1852 near Lodz in Russian Poland, of Austrian and German descent. His father had two sons from a first marriage and ten children from a second marriage, including my grandfather.

The Lange family had a flax textile mill on a large estate. Robert was 21 when he came to this country but took one or two trips back to Europe before he came west. At some point the older brother took over the textile business, so I suppose Robert came to this country looking for his fortune. Someone in the family, according to our family history, made a half million dollars on an invention to tie thread when making fabric. This process was patented in England. I don't think Robert shared in that windfall, unless that was the origin of the funds that they had, as at least some of the family was well educated.

Robert had a brother who was head of the Petrograd schools (St. Petersburg, Russia). He spoke eight (8!) languages fluently. The title of Excellency was bestowed upon this brother by the Czar because of his brilliance. Also, Robert's sister graduated from the University of Petrograd and was qualified to teach anywhere in Russia. Five children of the Lange family settled in the U.S.

My grandmother, Minnie Foron Lange, had French Canadian parents. When Minnie's mother, Mary Odile Lanceaux, was ten, she came west about 1858 with her family on the Oregon Trail from Kankakee, Illinois, in a covered wagon. They met mostly friendly Indians and gave each some hardtack cakes. At one place the chief's daughter took a liking to Mary's half-brother, Alfonce Lanceaux. He could have stayed and been the chief's son-in-law, but the idea did not appeal to him.

Three weeks before reaching Oregon City they ran out of food. They met some soldiers and traveled together the rest of the way. Grandmother's parents bought property at 10th and Washington in Portland. There were trees and brush between there and First Street, which was the main street at that time.

When Mary was sixteen, she married John Foron from Quebec. The Forons settled at Ford's Prairie near Centralia. They received a grant for this land signed by President Lincoln. Some time during that early period they lived for three weeks on wild strawberries with cream and sugar on biscuits.

Minnie Foron was their third child, with eight more to come after her.

In 1889 Minnie married Robert Lange and they settled in Toledo. He was 37 and a man of the world. She was 17 and right off the farm. According to my Aunt Lillian's history, they spent their honeymoon picking hops near Tacoma. They also lived in Chehalis and Castle Rock. They had five children—Lillian, Julia, Georgia, Emil and Teddy (who died when he was a young man).

General Mine Information

According to *The St. Helens Mining District* by R.H. McClure of the Forest Service, the first discoveries of mineral-bearing rock deposits were made in 1891 by Andy Olson, a farmer who was on a hunting and fishing trip. Between 1892 and 1911, over 400 mining claims were filed in the Spirit Lake and Green River area. The principal minerals were copper, gold and silver. Packers operated along the North Fork of the Toutle River and also along the Green River to reach the mines, as there was no road into the area.

McClure's report goes on as follows: "An account in the *Chehalis Nugget* reported that it is a settled fact that it is one of the richest districts that has been discovered since the palmy days of '49 when the great gold fields of California were first made known to the civilized world."

McClure states that among the better-financed claims were those of Dr. Henry Coe of Portland, who owned the Alaska Sanatorium. He had the Norway and Sweden Mines, with the Sweden Mine part way around the lake beyond Harmony Falls. These were Andy Olson's original claims purchased by Coe about 1900. And, in 1906, *The Advocate* mentions that Andy Olson was the foreman of Dr. Coe's mine at Spirit

Believed to be Andy Olson, Winthrop Rowe, Eugene Connolly

Lake. The Sweden camp was a large one with 15 buildings and employing 40 men. It was the only claim to have its ore removed and smelted. It was financed by selling shares of stock. Theodore Roosevelt was one of the shareholders. In 1905 some 13 tons of ore were transported across Spirit Lake by barge and then by wagon to Castle Rock.

The copper was used in the statue of Sacajawea now in Washington Park in Portland. Also, 10,000 souvenir spoons commemo-

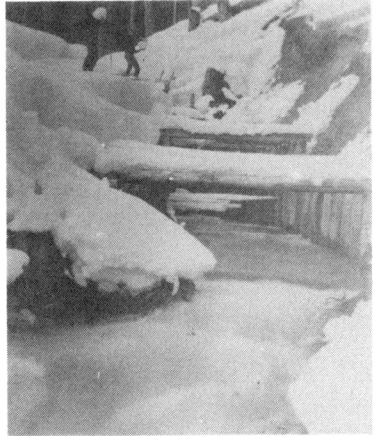

Coe's Dam (or Brown's Dam) at the outlet of Spirit Lake

rating the Lewis and Clark Exposition were made from the copper. Additional ore was removed for experimental smelting in 1929.

The Advocate of September 19, 1907, states: "We are informed that a dam is being built in Spirit Lake that is calculated to raise the waters at least ten feet, and much fear is felt by the people that should the

Brown's cabin, west side of cement bridge at the outlet. The cabin was gone by the time of the cement bridge.

dam break at any time, the whole Toutle region would be devastated by the rush of waters that would come down." Well, the dam was built, but no such mishap occurred. I have heard it called Coe's dam, but my mother had pictures that identified it as Brown's dam. As far as we know, in 1994 Jackson says the dam was commonly known as Coe's dam. It was located at the outlet of Spirit Lake. Mother also had a picture of a cabin down the Toutle River below the lake that she identified as Brown's cabin. Mr. Haynes, in his memoirs, stated that Coe had a sawmill about 1000 feet downstream of the dam. The water level of the lake was raised 5 or 6 feet as a result of the dam.

Lange's Mine

Mary Whitney—This is what Harry Gustafson, son-in-law of Robert Lange, said of Robert after many conversations with him in the 1920s.

"R.C. Lange was the first pioneer in this district. He was one of those rugged old pioneers who played a big part in making this the great country that it is today. Besides having a fine education, he traveled extensively throughout Europe and America in his younger days and could speak several languages. As a mining engineer and a mineralogist, he came to this beautiful wilderness in 1895. After considerable

Probably Lange's mine buildings

Blacksmith shed and bunkhouse at the Lange mine

time and hardship exploring this region with his riding and pack horses, he discovered and filed on several mining claims, mostly copper and a sprinkling of gold and silver. He formed a stock company and named it the Spirit Lake Mining and Power Company. The old-timers know it as the Lange Mines."

In my reading of several articles about the mines and family oral history, I learned of his two trips to Europe to receive financing for his mines. And I believe he received between $75,000 and $200,000 from German investors. Harold Samuelson said of his mine, "Lange's Mine, about one hour's hike above the lake, is today a half-filled hole in a vertical rock wall next to a cascading waterfall. The climber's tired foot stumbles over the remnants of narrow-gauge tracks that must have carried hand cars full of rock out of the mine. Panting from the climb, we

Grandpa's mill pond and flume

wonder how these miners managed to get their equipment up, and their rocks down, the incline. No level piece of ground is in sight anywhere."

I made this trip when I was about twelve, and we reached it from a trail that started from the Longview YMCA Camp, located on the roadless north side of the lake. I have a picture that would indicate there was a flume coming down the hill to carry water to his water wheel below and to furnish power to the mine and saw mill. *(Or was it a trestle for ore cars?—one of Leland Jackson's comments)*

The trestle (or flume) for the water wheel, vicinity of the Lange mine

R.C. Lange's one-man sawmill & log pond

Rollway to Lange's mill

L to R: Helper, another helper, Mr. Coe, Grandpa Lange, Grandma Lange, Mr. Wyler

Fire Story—probably circa 1908

Georgia Lange McCoy—A crown fire started on the ridge between Dr. Coe's and Lange's Mine. Burning whole logs and glowing embers rolled down the steep hillside and into the small creek from Minnie Falls, I believe, and stopped there. Luckily, none stopped over the mine opening.

We crossed the lake with Papa to help him and the young man he'd picked up. The young man was taken along to help pack the boxes of powder dynamite into the mine tunnel. The powder came from the powder house, which we would reach just before the camp. Papa had us halt some distance back before we reached the powder house while he went ahead to check the location of the fire. He wanted to see if there was any danger the fire had come near the powder house, also to see if there was a safe passageway from the powder house to the mine. Apparently there was, as we accomplished the move in about two hours.

Mine Story

Mary Whitney—The slopes still show the ravages of a gigantic forest fire started in 1908 by Lange's Mine workers, who lighted smudges to keep tormenting flies off their horses.

Harold Samuelson of the Forest Service, in a 1954 article, stated that the Cascades never had a gold rush anywhere near the California dimensions. People had been trying for years after the original mining rush to find their fortunes.

One mine, besides the large mines, was a one-man operation about 2½ miles below the homestead, operated by a man named Wyler. I don't know when he started, but he is pictured in a group in front of the sawmill along with Grandpa and Grandma Lange, Mr. Coe and helpers. Wyler was still around working that mine when I was there about 1930. So that was quite a span of time. Most of the mines ceased operations about 1911, so I don't know if Coe was included.

When I was up there, probably in 1945, there were horses and a packer on the homestead. This packer was to supply miners at the Polar Star Mine. We were on our way to the mine and met them coming out. So, I suppose that was a failure, too.

From *The Advocate*, March 18, 1937: "The rock crusher of William R. King, who is getting out crushed gravel from the Toutle River at Camp 502 for Weyerhaeuser, was damaged when a 140-pound nugget of almost pure copper was dropped into it while excavating from a gravel bar. The nugget had undoubtedly lodged in the bar after being washed down the Toutle from copper deposits in the Spirit Lake or Green River areas."

So, there *were* minerals. But, who knows if some of the transportation plans could have been carried out in the early days, and, if WWI hadn't intervened, then perhaps someone would have made a fortune.

Some Proposals Or Projects That Didn't Make It

The Advocate, December 9, 1897: "Mr. R.C. Lange, recorder of the St. Helens Mining District, was down from Toledo last week in the interest of a wagon road from Castle Rock to Spirit Lake, at the foot of Mt. St. Helens. The road is now open as far as the St. Helens post office, near Hoffstadts. And, if the county will establish and survey an extension from there to the eastern county line—which has now been surveyed by the government surveyors—the settlers, miners and all others interested in the opening of this much-needed public improvement will chip in and open the road. This will connect Castle Rock with one of the finest summer resorts in the Pacific Northwest."

The Advocate, January 11, 1906: "Wayne Stuart and Judge Rowan returned from a trip out on the route of the proposed Loop Line to Mt. St. Helens and reported having splendid success in securing right-of-way deeds."

The Advocate, August 25, 1907: "About the merriest crowd that has left this city for the mountains this summer started to Spirit Lake Monday morning. Chartering one of Plinny Shepardson's biggest teams and wagons, they loaded it to overflowing with camp equipage and good things to eat and merrily wended their way over the hills in the direction of their goal, all afoot save Mrs. Brewer and Louis Pauley, the driver. Those who comprise the party are Mrs. R. Brewer, Mrs. E.G. Rogers, Misses Helen Brewer, Gertrude Randall, Agnes Hansen, and Messers Percy Arthur, Ben Dixon, Ed Burt, John Pauly and Clifford Hogan."

The Advocate, August 2, 1908: "On Sunday morning, August 2, Mr. J.A. Byerly, of this city, accompanied by his son, Oliver, and William Teasley and G.F. McClane started to Spirit Lake in Mr. Byerly's Pope-Hartford touring car. It had been freely predicted that it was an impossibility for an automobile to reach the lake, but Mr. Byerly is a man of indomitable will as well as untiring energy who stops at neither labor nor expense when he desires to accomplish anything.

"So, the start was made with a mountain of supposed difficulties to face. Leaving this city at 6:40, the run was made to Silver Lake in 28 minutes, a distance of a little less than 7 miles. From there to Gardner's store, a little over 9 miles, the distance was covered in 22 minutes. At Gardner's some time was lost in filling up the gasoline tank and waiting for Mr. G. to appear in order to make a few minor purchases which were overlooked before starting. On over Green Mountain excellent time was made. St. Helen was reached a little after 10 o'clock, and high hopes were entertained that the lake would be reached by 3 o'clock.

"Although two of the party had been over the road before, they had not noticed the thousands of stumps which infested the middle of the road from about 2 miles beyond St. Helen all the way to the lake. Axes and mattocks were in almost constant use the remainder of the day, with the result that darkness found the party still 2 miles from Chipmunk Camp, which was their destination.

"Camp was made for the night near one of the finest springs of water that ever gushed from the bosom of Mother Earth. Daylight next morning found the party astir, but the stumps were still ahead of us. However, they were not as numerous as they were the day before, and good time was made until the big spring about a mile from camp was reached.

"Owing to the fact that a large boulder lay in the middle, making it impossible to run straight across, the machine was warped around it, but by the time it reached the other side, where there was a steep bank, the engines were so full of water and the gasoline so low that little power was left. The machine stuck and had to be hauled out with horses. From there on, good time was made to camp, as the remaining stumps had been chopped out in the meantime. Mr. Byerly, by his enterprise, had demonstrated that by the expenditure of a few hundred dollars a road could be made to the lake over which automobiles could easily make the round trip in a day of ten hours."

The Advocate, June 30, 1910: "A syndicate of capitalists has made a bonafide offer to furnish funds to the amount of one million dollars with which to construct an electric railway between Castle Rock and Mt. St. Helens and Spirit Lake. The road will also pass through some of the finest timber, much of which is mature and should be brought out as soon as possible after rail transportation is available."

The Advocate, August 7, 1913: "To anyone not having visited the

Spirit Lake and Mt. St. Helens country in the past three years, the great difference in the road's condition will be to them a great surprise and pleasure. Today you can drive an auto 25 to 30 miles an hour with perfect ease and safety. To drive an auto four or so years ago was practically impossible, having many sand pits to plow through, boulders and pumice-stone ridges to climb over, and the fording of the Toutle River in one or two instances. Now it is different. Suspension bridges span the river, and graded and widened roads take the place of the old road bed. The last 8 miles are particularly good, which heretofore have been the most difficult."

The Advocate, June 15, 1915: "Representatives of the Cascadia Mining Co. with extensive copper and other mining interests on Green River, about 6 miles northwest of Spirit Lake, came before the county commissioners this week asking for a survey of a first-class road route up the Toutle River and Green River so they could arrange to team their ore out to the railway. At present, the road goes over Green Mountain, making a heavy hauling charge. The company has more than 30,000 tons of ore and wishes to get it to market while the present high price for copper continues."

In 1916 John Burgoyne, also in Green River, contracted with a Portland engineer to construct a railroad up the Green River. The involvement of the U.S. in WWI prevented the plans from being carried out.

The Advocate, May 10, 1917: "County Commissioners Pete Laughlin, Al Mauer and F.M. Lane went out to Toutle Tuesday to look over the ground to put in a new road to Spirit Lake which will eliminate Green Mountain. The work will probably be done this summer."

The Advocate, August 1, 1929: "The road to Spirit Lake and Mt. St. Helens is declared to be in excellent condition now, according to reports of Castle Rock people who have recently made the trip. Repair work by the Forest Service on the last few miles of the road, and by Tom Cunningham's county crew on sections this side of the Eight-mile Bridge, has improved the road surface so that travel is made much easier.

"New decking has been placed on some of the old bridges, replacing the split cedar floors. Road crews from District Three are working on portions of the road beyond Kid Valley.

"The route to the lake is now by way of the Coal Bank Road, which is in excellent condition. This new road has cut down the mileage to the lake and provides a much safer and quicker route than the old one by way of Green Mountain. The trip from the lake to Castle Rock has been made in less than two hours, though that is faster than the average trip can be made. The trip to the lake from here can now be made in less than three hours."

The Homestead

Georgia Lange McCoy—About 1901, Papa petitioned the county commissioners of both Skamania and Cowlitz Counties to put in the upper half of the road to Spirit Lake so he could drive in with machinery and supplies for the mine and to bring his family in. Later, he was appointed road supervisor for Skamania County to put in the first Timberline Road from Spirit Lake.

Mary Whitney—Grandpa had built a small cabin on a bluff at the turn of the Toutle River a mile below Spirit Lake, later called the Original Homestead Cabin. This cabin was actually still in use in 1980 when the mountain blew. It had been remodeled several times. *The Advocate* said he was one of the first to offer tourist accommodations. He had camping space at his home, and boats which he rented to fishermen.

The Yacolt Fire, 1902

Georgia Lange McCoy—During the time of the fire, Papa was visited at the Homestead by a group of huckleberry pickers on horseback from the other side of the mountain. They had left their rigs and wagons near Yacolt, coming along the trail on the west side of Mt. St. Helens. There was no road on the South Toutle to the berry fields on the north side. My father tried his best to persuade them not to go back the way they came; if there would be a change in direction of the wind, they wouldn't have a chance. They decided to chance it to save their wagons and buggies, but that is history. They were caught in the forest fire which became known as the "Yacolt Burn" and perished. A few of the horses that broke away and made a run for it made it to safety. Papa just seemed to know things without having experienced them.

Our First Family Trip

Georgia Lange McCoy—May 18, 1900, to May 18, 1903—Teddy was three years old when the family went to the mountain the first time. I was left at Grandma's farm at Toledo because I was still motion-sick in the morning, after the trip from Chehalis the day before. So, the family left without me. I was eight years old that summer. I had to wait until the summer after the next summer because the family missed going that year. I was anxious to go after all the tall stories I had heard when the family arrived home. The route from Chehalis was via Toledo and Grandfather's farm and then to Spirit Lake. It was a 3½ day trip in. The stay at the farm was not without its compensations. I saw the grapevines growing for the first time, though I was not there for the harvest. The red raspberries were delicious.

Mary Whitney—My mother has said she walked most of the way on those trips. A wagon ride would certainly not help motion sickness, so she did a lot of walking in those days.

Forest Fire Musings

Georgia Lange McCoy—Ashes falling in the clearing in the very early days. No transportation on hand—would have to be able to get to the lake and across to the old mine scow and move that to the opposite site from the faster-burning area. These things we kids discussed among ourselves. One time the mine landing blew up from glycerin-saturated walls where boxes of powder were stacked. It blew the man, who struck the lighted match, through the door. At least he wasn't injured.

Mine Story—The German Engineer

Georgia Lange McCoy—When Lilly was in her middle teens, we went across the lake and up to the mines—that steep 1¼ or so miles up to the mill and cluster of buildings, crossing a little stream, and then to the mine opening in the hillside. At this time we had a German engineer at the mine, sent over at the insistence of the German stockholders. The method used in Germany was to drill a small tunnel—instead of the generous one in which you could stand upright with space to spare. The engineer was a supercilious man, wearing white spats, shiny boots, a trim uniform of some sort, and carrying a cane. His military training was evident—swinging his cane as he paced back and forth on a log lying alongside the road across from the cook house and dining room. Lilly and I were to eat our noon meal there, and the engineer gallantly had his silver set at her place at the table.

Mary Whitney—By 1911 most of the miners had given up, although there were some exceptions. Grandpa Lange still hadn't given up according to two *Advocate* articles. On October 10, 1911, it mentions he was on his way to Spirit Lake where he was having a road built around the lake to his mine. (I believe it only extended a short way beyond the Portland YMCA.) The second article on December 14, 1911, said they were informed that he had bought up the conflicting interests in his mines and was now prepared to go ahead with developing the properties.

I don't know what happened after that, but I believe he might have done a little work, but not in an organized way. This is what Harry Gustafson said, "After spending a small fortune developing these mines and due to the lack of funds, transportation, and many other hardships, the venture went on the rocks like so many ventures of the early pioneers."

I believe the Lange family blamed the failure of the mine partly on the German engineer, as there were many stories about him. He was utterly out of place in that rugged territory.

While Grandpa was traveling in Europe to find financing for his mines, Grandma Lange was busy raising five children. Among the many trips he took was one to a reunion, probably in Missouri, of some of his

Lange family siblings. Three brothers and a sister who settled in the United States were there, along with a brother who returned to Europe and a sister whose whereabouts remain a mystery. *(mw)*

Patent Problems

Georgia Lange McCoy—Papa, when his claim for the homestead was turned down by the Department of Interior, took his case directly to the President and won it. He had to clear 5 acres and grow food.

Mary Whitney—From *The Advocate*, August 25, 1910: "R.C. Lange was in town for a short time while on his way to face the government in their attempt to take his homestead from him. Mr. Lange had filed long before the Spirit Lake region was made a Forest Reserve, and it seems like it would be rank injustice to take the land away from him, particularly in view of the fact that he has expended much money in improving it, and years of hard work." Also, *The Advocate* said the late Senator Wesley L. Jones was helpful.

Rick Lange, at Emil's memorial service in January 1992, related some of the mountain stories Emil had told him. One was that Grandpa Lange took a stalk of oats that he had grown on the homestead to the President and won his case. That certainly makes sense, as I don't believe there were meadows or grazing for horses at that time. Since horsepower was all they had, it would have meant a tremendous amount of feed to transport up there.

From *The Advocate* of October 23, 1913: "R.C. Lange and wife, of the towns of Chehalis and Lange, Washington, came in from the latter place on their way to their winter home at Chehalis. Mr. Lange had a smile on his face as long as a fence rail because of the fact that he had recently received word from Washington that Secretary Lane ordered that a patent be granted to Mr. Lange for his homestead at Spirit Lake.

The patent was granted March 27, 1914, under an act of Congress May 20, 1862, and signed by President Woodrow Wilson.

Five acres had to be cleared to "prove up" on the homestead.

A very-early-day road

Front of the second or third homestead building

Georgia and Julia Lange in back of the homestead building, about 1915

Lange family about 1908 or 1910

Northern Pacific cruisers ready to climb Mt. St. Helens, Georgia Lange at front, left

On Timberline Road (Note fender of car, left front)

Cataboo Cabin, near the outlet of Spirit Lake—Georgia Lange by door

Interior of Cataboo Cabin, which was Lillian Lange's store at the outlet—later, Harry Truman's location

Community

Mary Whitney—The Portland YMCA became a factor in the settling of the Mt. St. Helens area. Mr. J.C. Meehan, who later became general secretary of the Portland Y, was an early leader up there. In my mother's collection of memorabilia is a copy of a 1908 *Prospectus for a Mazama Annual Outing* that had Mr. Meehan's name written on top. At some period he had worked with a survey crew for the Northern Pacific Railway. One of my mother's early pictures was taken about 1912 with Mr. Meehan as the leader of a group of campers. It was really a community in those days. Emil and Teddy swam and hiked with the Y boys. Lillian, Julia and Georgia climbed the mountain with N.P. cruisers and families—also maybe with some of the other homesteaders or Castle Rock boys.

Lillian's Store At The Lake

Mary Whitney—My mother had several pictures of Lillian's store, called Cataboo Cabin, at the outlet of the lake. This was near the spring on what became Harry Truman's place. This store was a log cabin and it doesn't say who built it. The buildings Grandpa built were of lumber from his mill, but this must have been an earlier time, when the mine was still in operation. I say this because that was the landing they used when they brought the ore over. My mother, in her notes, mentions several homesteaders: W.V. Hyde, Wakefield, Eugene Connolly, Andy Olson and brother Winthrop Rowe—maybe 10-14 miles down the road. She didn't finish her notes on the above. Following is what she said about an early pioneer:

Gratia Huntington—Castle Rock Pioneer

Georgia Lange McCoy—Gratia Huntington, a resident of Castle Rock, once told me that as a young girl with tuberculosis her folks sent her up to the foot of Mt. St. Helens. Gratia said they went up on horseback and had to ford the river six or seven times, as there were no roads or bridges. She was 75 years old at the time she spoke of it to me. Her brother was Luther Huntington, who had a tourist cabin camp by the river near the Kalama bridge. Earlier, we kids knew him when he had a "tent" store and boat rental on the shore of Spirit Lake. We rented his shell boats many times in the summer to row over to Harmony Falls. This was years before Jack Nelson's Harmony Falls lodge and cabins were there. Our favorite places to row were Bear Creek and Coe's Mine.

Building & The Sawmill

Mary Whitney—I believe that with his sawmill Grandpa Lange was very instrumental in the growth of the Spirit Lake region. To my knowledge, most of the buildings used lumber from that sawmill, although there were some log cabins built also. The lumber was used from the little one-room original homestead cabin to the last store building, which included a restaurant, post office and living quarters. This building was built in the late 1920s and I spent ten summers in it. Grandpa also built a two-part structure with a breezeway, as well as a "hotel." In 1916 he platted a townsite which he called The Pines. He had picture letterheads of his hotel, The Old Homestead, along with other scenic views of the mountain country. There were four residences built in all on the homestead property, plus rental cabins.

The Pines Hotel and townsite, platted 1916

Letterhead of The Pines. (Note: Address is Lange, Wash.)

The Sunday Oregonian, July 25, 1926: "One-man Sawmill Cuts 1000 Feet Daily under Ex-prospector's Expert Guidance." The article included a picture titled "R.C. Lange's one-man sawmill near Spirit Lake, Mt. St. Helens." The quotation read, "Probably the only *one-man* sawmill in the Pacific NW, if not in the world. Lange built the mill without the assistance of anyone else and is operating it alone by means of a primitive waterwheel. He has been furnishing lumber for the YMCA Camp and also for the government road builders in his vicinity. He can start his mill by pulling a single lever. This action directs the water from a nearby stream into a sluice and starts his wheel turning. A long iron shaft runs from the waterwheel and is connected to his saw by a pulley. All the mill operations must be done very carefully as the mill building is getting old and its foundations are rotting. Whenever the mill building is jarred, the pilings on one side settle and operations must cease until the building is jacked up level again." Pictures of the sawmill in operation were taken by *The Oregonian* and were shown at the Rivoli Theater.

Also, there was a short movie or newsreel made comparing the huge Long Bell Mill at Longview with his one-man sawmill.

As I think of Grandpa's sawmill, I remember playing on the logs stored in front of the mill waiting to be sawn—also, rowing around in a boat in the millpond, which was released when logs were to be sawn. But, after I started spending summers up there, I don't remember activity at the mill and believe the snow broke it down in the early 1930s.

Leased Land

The Advocate, July 10, 1913: "Louis Pauly, who returned from Spirit Lake Thursday, reports that he had a horrible trip, as it rained about all the time and the roads were in a terrible condition. He said that E.S. Collins of Ostrander and Fred Taylor of Kelso were there with their autos, fixing up their very elaborate summer camps. Senator Stewart is also going to fix up a camp there. They are all putting up cottages on land leased from the government." (I don't know if this was ever realized.)

The Advocate, March 27, 1919: "A survey, which includes 41 summer sites, one hotel and a public campground on the shore of Spirit Lake, has been approved by District Forester George Cecil. This is the second group of summer sites to be surveyed and is about ½ mile west of the YMCA Camp." There were several cabins built near the Y—the Crums', Bradleys', and a cabin occupied by the Meehans when they were at the lake. Later, the Meehans built their lovely cabin across the lake on the north side.

Mr. Haynes said his father built their cabin in 1923 on Forest Service leased land using lumber from Grandpa Lange's sawmill. It was located near to what later became Jack Nelson's telephone and landing (to pick up his guests).

There were stringent restrictions regarding the leases. Mr. Haynes said that after his father died, and when his mother could no longer use it, they had to tear the cabin down and leave the site in its original condition. Perhaps that is what happened to the earlier leases, especially those close to the camp.

Other Developments & Happenings

The Advocate, June 8, 1911: "H.V. Huntington returned from taking a load of freight as far as the 8-mile post and reported that wolves are very numerous in that region. Chicken and other fowl frequently have fallen prey to them. Also, elk are being rapidly decimated by the wolves."

Phones

One *Advocate* item dated May 15, 1913, mentions Grandpa Lange fixing the telephone lines in the spring. We actually had telephone service to Castle Rock in those days. I have wondered who fixed the lines in the spring when he was no longer able to do it. It seems to me Harold Samuelson also worked on the line. Later, in more modern times so to speak, there was no phone service to town. If you wanted to make a reservation for a cabin, you had to write. But in the ten years I was up there, we had phone service. I suppose when the road was finished on the north side of the Toutle that could have been the end of the line.

In the winter the Langes lived in Chehalis. Grandma's two brothers had a coal mine in Centralia and Grandpa worked there as a bookkeeper. At some period before 1920 the family lived in Castle Rock, as that was where my mother graduated.

R.C. (Grandpa) & Minnie (Grandma) Lange

Harry and Julia (Lange) Gustafson and the first log cabin that they built

Grandma Lange, Harry Gustafson, & Grandpa Lange

Papa Versus You-Know-Who & Other Family Memories

Georgia Lange McCoy—Papa never had to use all those cuss-word adjectives like some to get attention. If he didn't like something we kids had done, he just let out a bellow like an enraged bull and hollered, "Donner vetter know a mile!" (Roughly translated: Thunder weather is here again!) And if he didn't believe something—"Poppy cock!"

Mary Whitney—Mamma got used to his big voice and his way of showing he was on the job. At the mountains she could very well have depended, I believe, on Papa's sonic booms to scare the cougars from attacking them when they went out with lanterns at night. She could have dispensed with beating a tin pie plate with a metal spoon. This enraged Papa.

In later years Mamma was given the nickname of *Cougar Min* by Bessie Meehan. But, don't get the idea from that that she didn't have courage, because she did. She would have fought to the death for any of us. I have seen her wade into a dog fight that had got out of hand, and she knew all the consequences. Her fears, thinking in advance, were worse than facing the real thing. She had another nickname, too. She didn't seem to mind. When we were a lot smaller than her *Cougar Min* nickname, she was called *Ozone, the Fresh-air Crusader*. That just fit her, as she would go out every chance she had to get fresh air.

Mamma was great—almost one of *us*. God bless her!

The Decade of The 1920s

Mary Whitney—The 1920 Portland census showed Grandpa Lange as working in a Portland shipyard as a machinist—at the age of 68.

Sometime, probably in the 1920s, Grandpa Lange mortgaged half of his 160 acres to Julia and Harry Gustafson. Summer homestead earnings probably provided only summer living, and eventually Grandma and Grandpa spent winters at Harry and Julia's. The mortgage was to build the new store building which, I believe, was built in the late 1920s.

1924 & Sasquatch

Possibly the news that generated more publicity than any other, until the mountain blew, was the report of a miner's cabin at the bottom of a canyon, being attacked from above by four hairy creatures. Huge footprints were supposed to have been found. Many stories have been written and several people have claimed credit for these. Anyhow, it was a good story and resulted in the naming of Ape Canyon.

Enter Harry Truman

From several "Advocate" articles—

"In 1928 Articles of Incorporation were filed by James Menane and others with capital stock of $50,000 to lease 40 acres at Harmony Falls with 2,000-foot frontage on the lake, property being owned by the Coe estate. The purpose is to operate resort facilities—including a park, hotel, cabins and boats—to furnish guide service and to sell supplies. R.C. Lange will cut rough lumber that is needed for the hotel and other buildings. Another development at Spirit Lake this year is the Holmstedt Memorial Building, under construction by the YMCA."

October 3, 1929: "The St. Helens Lodge is in the charge of Jack Nelson and Harold Samuelson, who will remain there all winter."

October 17, 1929: "On his way home from a hunting trip to Spirit Lake, the car of Harry Truman of Chehalis turned over on the road near Kid Valley. The sedan rolled over at least twice. A wheel came off causing the accident. Truman was alone in the car. Jack Nelson of the Mt. St. Helens Lodge at Spirit Lake was notified of the accident, and he drove the 25 miles from the lake to take Truman on to Chehalis. It was found that his injuries were not serious."

March 27, 1930: "Jack Nelson announced that he had sold his interest in the Mt. St. Helens Lodge at Spirit Lake to Harry Truman of Chehalis, who has been his partner since last fall. Mr. Nelson started the resort over two years ago and operated it for two seasons. He built cabins, a store and lodge, and added to a fleet of rowboats, so that there are now 21 at the camp, besides two launches. Truman, formerly a Chehalis garage operator, will take charge at once. Nelson's plans for the future are uncertain, he stated."

By July 1930, Jack Nelson was operating Harmony Falls Park. So began the long saga of resort ownership (and competition at the lake), with the Langes a poor third. They probably didn't consider us competition because we just got the overflow when the other cabins were rented.

The Homestead In My Day

Mary Whitney—I was sent to the homestead in 1929 at age ten, partly to be baby-sat, and partly to help out, as Grandma and Grandpa were running the store and restaurant and renting cabins. Also, Grandpa had the post office. My dad, Kelsey McCoy, died when I was six, and I had a series of baby-sitters. I spent ten summers up there.

The Store Building

Mary Whitney—The building at that time was quite new. It was probably built in 1928 and the last that Grandpa built. The front had windows all around, and it had a restaurant and store in front, with counters and shelves at the back of the room. In back of that was the kitchen, a combination living/bedroom, and the little post office, where I slept.

We had a few modern conveniences in the old store building—running water (which you had to keep running 24 hours a day to keep sand from blocking the pipe at the spring), hot water, and a shower-room attached to the house but reached by going outside. At one point a generator was there for electric lights, but that was not very successful and was soon discarded. We also had a cooler, which was in a little shed by the kitchen door, and it had spring water running through it.

The road to the lake ran directly in front of the store.

I've always wished I could have heard the stories Grandpa Lange told. I always did think he was probably more interesting than Harry

Truman. He had the perfect opportunity with the restaurant and the store to talk to people. But I don't think I got to hear any of his stories because when I had finished clearing the tables I was back in the kitchen washing dishes.

In 1929 Grandpa received a permit to operate a post office which was to be open six months a year. The place was kept open through the November elections.

The Depression

Mary Whitney—Those years were, of course, The Depression—and I don't know how much difference that made in our business. The worst time that I remember was a 4th of July when we only sold four chicken dinners, and that was all we served that whole day. I don't remember if it was because of rain or The Depression, or both. The resorts needed good weather for the 4th and Labor Day particularly, in order to survive. It just seemed like the weather didn't cooperate very much on those weekends. Also, if the other resorts didn't get filled, we were out of luck. Of course, almost all of the tourists wanted to stay at the lake.

I think that at times our cabins were rented to road workers and others who wanted to stay on a weekly or monthly basis—also some people who couldn't afford the prices at the lake.

I wasn't aware of The Depression as much out there. We had

Older homestead buildings, Lilly's cabin behind the big store building, gas building across the "street"

The last store building built by Grandpa Lange, about 1926-28

plenty of food and Grandpa had somewhat expensive tastes. We had strawberries and cream from town even when ours weren't bearing. Those were the years when you charged groceries at the store.

For the restaurant, Grandpa cooked the meat—probably mostly beef roast for sandwiches. He gathered mushrooms in the fall and made rich gravies. Grandma made huckleberry pies, but usually we didn't get to eat them until they were about a week old—just in case there were customers. Couldn't do that with today's pies!

I remember a little about the day Grandpa Lange died, either late November or early December 1933. He and Grandma had been down

Winter at the store building

to Harry Truman's at Studebaker, about 3½ miles down, and Harry gave them chili for lunch. Grandma thought it was the chili that had given Grandpa his heart attack. Truman, Lige Coalman, his son, and Sam were the ones who rigged some

Snow-flattened store with the woodshed and Lilly's cabin in back, probably 1948-50

kind of stretcher and ropes tied on each side of Dry Gulch (which was in flood stage) and worked their way across. Then they had to carry him farther because of road washouts. That was the beginning of one of the worst floods Castle Rock had. Possibly it happened a week or two later.

This flood also set the Spirit Lake road back, as they had to re-build portions instead of just continuing from where the last contract had been completed.

After Grandpa Lange died, my mother either gave up her job or took a leave from the post office to help run the place. She worked out there for three summers and had to stay until the election was over in November. That meant that after school started I had to board and

Lorene Thomas (Lilly's daughter) and Grandma Lange at the store counter

room in Castle Rock and find a ride to the lake on weekends. So, three years was enough for us, and after that Julia Gustafson quit her job in Portland and ran the place.

The new road to the lake was probably finally finished in 1939-40. But, during the last year or so before the last mile was finished, the traffic came

Dry Gulch—was flooding in 1933 when Grandpa Lange died. He had to be hauled across the gulch to get to the road.

across a bridge and then through the bottom of our place before connecting to the existing road to the lake in front of our store.

Julia and Harry and various carpenters started building their Spirit Lake Lodge and were open when the road to the lake was finished. Julia died from breast cancer about 1942-43.

This is what Harry Gustafson had to say about Grandpa Lange: "Mr. Lange was always talking and dreaming of the future, too busy to ever think of the past. I have always known him as happy, rich or poor, and never worried or crossed his bridges before he came to them. He always seemed happiest when he could be around his children and younger folks. When I was a kid in my 20s, time and again we sat on the high bank across from the lodge and I would dream with him about his Castle on the Rhine, as he picturesquely described the lodge that he was someday planning to build. So, after he passed away, it was up to me to carry on with his beautiful dream of the Castle on the Rhine, which I named Spirit Lake Lodge."

Lange's first homestead cabin, built about 1902 on point of the river. This picture was taken about 1969. The cabin was remodeled later. This was Grandpa Lange's "Castle on the Rhine."

Auto-Stage To Spirit Lake, Washington

From "The Independent", 1917—

Mr. R.C. Lange announces that on Saturday, June 30, 1917, his auto will begin to make regular weekly trips between Castle Rock and Spirit Lake and Mt. St. Helens. Later on, the service will be extended.

With this Auto-Stage in operation, the general public will find a long-felt want filled and, no doubt, will make liberal use of it now that the regular summer season has set in and the people begin to look for cooler spots.

Parties intending to visit Spirit Lake this summer will do well to have their hotel accommodations and transportation booked before-hand, as over-crowding of the stage will be strictly avoided.

Special trips can be arranged and full information obtained by phone and round-trip tickets procured at the Castle Rock Garage. Make your reservations now.

R.C. Lange Rented Boats At Spirit Lake In 1902

Another notice in a paper—

One of the first to offer accommodations for tourists at Spirit Lake was R.C. Lange, who settled on a homestead there in 1902. He had camping space at his home and boats which he rented to fishermen.

Lange first became interested in the Spirit Lake region in 1901 while prospecting in the territory. He was living at Toledo at the time.

Cowlitz County opened a wagon road from Castle Rock to Spirit Lake in the winter of 1901-02, and when the road was opened in the spring, Lange moved to his wilderness home with his wife and five children.

Clearing away heavy underbrush and numerous windfalls to make a spot for his garden and crops was his first task in establishing a home.

Lange died in December 1933, at the age of 81.

The resort now is known as Spirit Lake Lodge and is owned and operated by Mr. and Mrs. Harry O. Gustafson. (Note: Mrs. Gustafson was Julia Lange Gustafson.)

The St. Helens Mining District—A Condensed History

by R.H. McClure, Jr., copyrighted in 1984 by "Skamania Co. Heritage"

The most prominent landmark of northwest Skamania County is, of course, Mt. St. Helens. In 1892 the name of the volcano was used to designate a 156-square-mile mining district with boundaries approximating the present zone of devastation resulting from the 1980 eruptive blast. Between 1892 and 1911, over 400 mining claims were filed for the area north of Spirit Lake—including the headwaters of the Green River. The principal minerals attracting prospectors to the area were copper, gold and silver.

As early as the 1850s, prospectors searching the upper Lewis River had reported gold in streams emptying into the present Swift Reservoir. Small amounts of gold were also found in the gravels of the Toutle River in following years. Nothing substantial developed out of these early prospects.

The first discoveries of mineral-bearing rock deposits were made in 1891 by Andy Olson, a farmer who entered the Spirit Lake area on a hunting and fishing trip. Word of the finds traveled quickly, and in the following year numerous mineral claims were staked on the Green River. Most of the claims were filed by individuals, but several companies were formed in the first year, setting a precedent for further development. It is apparent from early newspaper accounts that gold-seeking was the primary motivation behind the flurry of activity which characterized the first decade of work in the district.

An 1895 account in *The Chehalis Nugget* reported that "it is a settled fact that it is one of the richest districts that has been discovered since the palmy days of '49 when the great gold fields of California were first made known to the civilized world." Journalism of this sort no doubt played an important part in developing the financial backing necessary to organize companies, establish camps, and work the mines.

A developer named Ludluck oversaw construction of a camp near Ryan Lake (originally Rhine Lake) in about 1895 with the financial aid of a Milwaukee newspaper. Ludluck's company, the Milwaukee Pacific Mining and Exploration Company, was also responsible for a number of fairly-well-known Green River mines—including the Minnie Lee, Independence and Last Hope. Two of the original cabins built by this company, still standing in 1979, were flattened by the recent devastating eruption of Mt. St. Helens.

While almost all of the mining claims in the Mt. St. Helens Mining District were situated in Skamania County, merchants there received no benefit from the scores of miners flocking to the area. Access to the mines was by way of the Toutle River from such towns as Castle Rock and Toledo in neighboring Cowlitz County. Outfitters in these towns supplied the miners with clothing, axes, saws, horses, lamps, explosives, and groceries, as well as other tools specific to hard rock mining. Packers operated along the North Fork of the Toutle to Spirit Lake and along the Green River route. By 1901 the trail into Spirit Lake had been improved to a wagon road. In order to transport ore from the district, attempts to secure support for a railroad were made by several of the mining companies. These efforts were unsuccessful.

Among the better-financed mining operations were those of Dr. Henry Coe. Although Coe held claims throughout the district, most of his work centered on two mines near the north shore of Spirit Lake. The Norway and Sweden mines, as they were named, were on Olson's original claim, purchased by Coe about 1900. A large camp of some 15 buildings, employing 40 men, became the headquarters of Coe's Mt. St. Helens Consolidated Mining Company, and was located at the Sweden Mine. The explorations and developments of the company were financed by the selling of shares of stock. Theodore Roosevelt was one of the company stockholders and may also have had holdings in the previously mentioned Milwaukee Pacific Company.

The Sweden mine, now beneath the post-eruption water level of Spirit Lake, was the only claim in the mining district to have its ore removed and smelted. In 1905 some 13 tons were transported across Spirit Lake by barge and then by wagon 38 miles to Castle Rock. The copper extracted from this ore was incorporated into the statue of Sacagawea unveiled as a part of Portland's Lewis and Clark Exposition, and presently standing in Washington Park. Ten thousand souvenir spoons commemorating the Exposition were also made from this copper. Additional ore was removed from the 2800-foot Sweden tunnel for experimental smelting in 1929.

Although assay reports on the Sweden ore indicated new returns, taking into account freighting and treatment, of between 10 and 25 dollars per ton, this was not incentive enough for further transportation development. Most of the cabins and mines in the district were abandoned by 1911. Huge ore dumps at the mouths of many tunnels attested to the hundreds of thousands of dollars of investors' money that was spent on labor and simple development. With no prospect of road or rail access, most claimholders quit their work.

In 1916 John Burgoyne, a miner who had been active in the district since about 1900, contracted with a Portland engineer to construct a railroad up the Green River. Apparently, the involvement of the United States in World War I prevented the plans from being carried out. Between 1911 and 1916 virtually all development had been on the Green River area claims of John Burgoyne and those of the Cascadia Mining and Development Company.

Among the mines of the latter were the Polar Star and Brooklyn, as well as holdings purchased from the earlier Milwaukee Pacific Company. World War I essentially ended activity in the mining district and, except for a small amount of exploration in the 1930s, the mineral de-

Harry Dutch (left) and Alex Burgoyne (right) pose with cedar shoring planks at the Black Prince Mine, St. Helens Mining District, in 1904.

posits were all but forgotten.

In the 1960s and 1970s two large southwestern mining corporations refiled on many of the old claims and conducted test drilling over much of the St. Helens Mining District. After the creation of the Mt. St. Helens National Volcanic Monument in 1982, many of the claims were voluntarily relinquished. Most of the district is on lands under the administration of the U.S. Forest Service which has, in recent years, been involved in a program to relocate and document the remains of the historic mines and camps.

This program has included archival research, archaeological survey, mapping, and some test excavation as means to understanding more about the history of this little-known mining district.

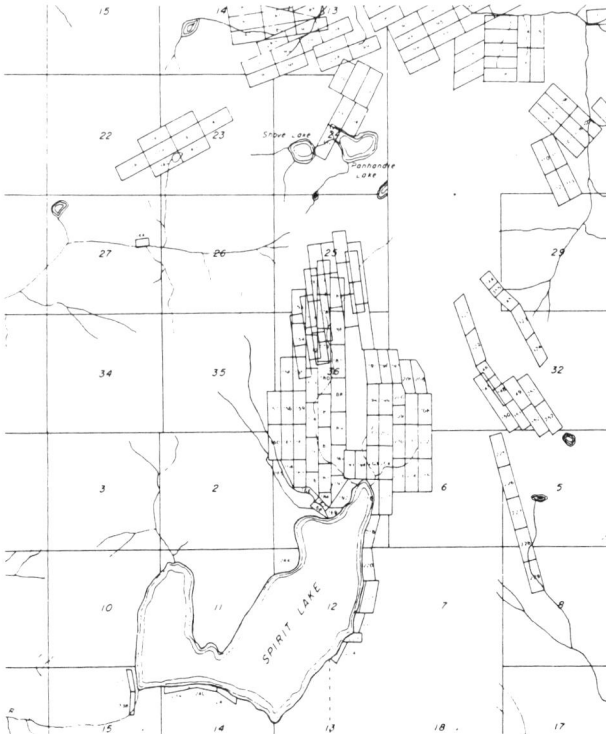

Spirit Lake and the Upper Green River Country. Numbered squares represent township sections, numbered rectangles designate individual mining claims. Adapted from Figure 20 of A Cultural Resource Overview of the Gifford Pinchot National Forest, South-Central Washington, 1976, by J.V Jermann and R.D. Mason.

St. Helens Mines

The Advocate (?), an unsigned story of January 1, 1896, St. Helens Valley: "This valley is in the northeastern part of Cowlitz County, lying along the north branch of the Toutle River. The valley is 1½ miles wide and 32 miles long, embracing 48 sections and about 32,000 acres of agriculture, timber and mineral lands. It extends east to the St. Helens mines. Gold was first discovered here about 1878, but little attention was given to that country until this year, when a number of ledges of pay ore were discovered. So late in the season were these discoveries made that there was no time for development. The country is thoroughly mineralized, almost solid mountains of quartz, the various assays ranging from $5 to $500 per ton. Extensive preparations are being made for future work. It is safe to predict that next year will develop rich and valuable properties. An electric railway up the valley is one of the propositions now under consideration and the opening of these mines will give this county an impetus that will sweep it on to one of the richest in the state."

Cowlitz County Historical Quarterly, Vol. IV, No. 2, P.17, August, 1962: "When the mines were opened up in the Mt. Helens country in 1897, freight increased enough to justify the Northwest making three trips a week again. Fares were $2 a round trip from Castle Rock to Portland, or $1.25 one way."

The Advocate, July 29, 1897: "C.M. Antrim returned Sunday from a couple of weeks' outing in the St. Helens mining district. He brought back a specimen or two of ore from the Spirit Lake mines that are very valuable-looking quartz."

The Advocate, October 7, 1897: "Joseph Price, while digging a well on his farm on the South Fork of the Toutle River a few days ago, ran into a 2-foot ledge of what proves by analysis to be pure copper. The ledge is of decomposed quartz and lays about 12 feet under ground."

The Advocate, July 4, 1907: "Three teams and wagons, loaded with a water wheel and other machinery for the power plant of the St. Helens, Oregon, Mill and Power Company on the Toutle River near Spirit Lake, left here for that point yesterday, and another will leave on

Friday, the 5th. The combined weight of the wheel and its necessary fittings was 7,000 pounds."

"Hollywood Gorge" on the Toutle River. Also known as the dam site. This was the area under consideration for a dam which would provide electricity for a railway up the valley. Note: This narrow spot is what saved Castle Rock and the rest of the downstream from more damage during the eruption of 1981.

Portland YMCA Boys' Camp at Spirit Lake

by M.D. Wilder, Assoc. General Secretary & former Longview resident

1959 marks the 75th anniversary of the initiation by a New York State YMCA of organized youth camping. A Y board member took the little group of seventeen boys from Newburgh out for ten days or so and was so impressed by the experience of an uninterrupted sojourn close to nature with a compact group of youth in their formative period that he wrote, prophetically, to the editor of a contemporary magazine: "I have just returned from one of the most profitable experiences of my life—I write you this because I think it may be a valuable feature of summer work with boys." His far-sighted view is borne out by the estimate that five million boys and girls will be enrolled in youth camps this summer.

The Portland YMCA began camping with boys about the turn of the century, the precise year is not quite certain. Camping was done on a somewhat *al fresco* basis, with no fixed site—for several years at the Pacific beach, and for some years at various locations up the Columbia River. In the meantime, about 1907, members of the Boys' Work Committee of the Portland YMCA, particularly Mr. E.S. Collins, were looking about, as they had opportunity, for a suitable site for permanent camping. Mr. Collins was familiar with the then remote Spirit Lake country, populated only by a few hopeful mining prospectors and timbermen, and he took the lead in urging J.C. Clark, then Boys' Work Secretary of the Portland Y, and J.C. Meehan, Mr. Clark's assistant, to settle their camping plans around Spirit Lake.

The first camp at the lake was conducted in 1909 under Mr. Clark's direction. The enterprise was wholly primitive camping—meals cooked over open camp fires, campers sleeping under canvas. The camp was pitched at about the present site of the large forest campground. During the following year Mr. Clark went to Shanghai, China, to become secretary for work with boys of the YMCA there, and Mr. Meehan assumed the direction of the camping program and continued to give it his personal direction until 1932, and his devoted oversight and interest until his death in 1948.

The first permanent site was secured by special use permit from the Forest Service about 1911. This is the location at the south end of the lake just east of the Ranger Station, which to 40 seasons of Y boy campers was the Spirit Lake Camp. The original building on this site was a log cabin which ultimately became the camp kitchen, and which in the early years was flanked by a similarly designed and constructed cabin some 40-feet distant; the two then being connected by the outdoor dining pavilion which has faced the lake through the years. The first permanent building, the Spirit Lake Lodge, was erected about 1913, and this became the activity and program headquarters of the camp, as well as the over-winter storage for foodstuffs and other supplies which were left on the site. These latter were built by boys in partnerships of two and three, and the shelters remained the property of some men who have since won prominence in business and the professions. The shelters remained the property of the builders as long as they continued to come to camp.

The death in 1926 of Charlie Holmstedt—a picturesque character who had from early days of the camp been the camp cook in summer and a caretaker and maintenance man in the winter—removed a colorful personage from the scene. Out of their great affection for him, a number of campers, parents and other friends built the monumental Holmstedt Memorial Lodge in 1928. This building—with its large unobstructed ground floor space, heated by enormous field stone fireplaces at either end, and containing a second-floor, guest-room space for 50 visitors—served as a camp community center until removal of YMCA camping in 1951 to the third and present site.

In the mid-1930s the sudden discovery of Spirit Lake by great numbers of the general public, and pressures to plan long-term recreational developments around the lake area, led to a strong suspicion that the large area developed by the Portland YMCA might be seriously curtailed or completely recovered by the Forest Service. The Association was very thoughtfully advised by its friends in the government agency to take precautionary measures against possible loss of its Spirit Lake camping, which by then was already becoming a legend. Accordingly, steps were initiated to acquire lake shore property by purchase, and in the late 1930s the present wooded area at the extreme north end of Spirit Lake was acquired from Dr. Henry Waldo Coe and his associates in the Coe copper mining venture.

The intervention of war years delayed any but the most preliminary development until 1946 when began construction of the present complex of sleeping quarters, dining lodge, director's residence, storage buildings, store, camera laboratory, craft lodge, sanitary buildings, power plant, and other facilities to house and provide service for 100 boys and their leaders. Plans for full development call for additional projects which will extend into another 5 to 10 years.

A feature which impresses both campers and visitors is the rustic Meehan Memorial Chapel, constructed entirely by boy campers and dedicated to the memory of the leadership of J.C. Meehan. Mr. Meehan was undoubtedly the guiding influence in the development and history of the camp, although he entered it as director in its second season. He

became General Secretary of the Portland YMCA in 1932 upon the re-
tirement of H.W. Stone, and at that time relinquished actual and im-
mediate direction to others on the YMCA staff, but he continued until
his death in 1948 his unremitting attention to it. He and Mrs. Meehan
were peculiarly part of the Spirit Lake community as it grew up. They
had long occupied residency there from May through December annu-
ally. On the 70th Anniversary of the Portland YMCA in 1938, the Board
of Directors surprised Mr. Meehan by officially naming the Spirit Lake
camp for him.

The development of the new campsite made possible the beginning of camping there, and for several years two units of camping were
conducted—older boys in a completely wilderness camping program
being located at the new site. In1951 a decision was taken to consoli-
date all boys' camping at the new Camp Meehan location. A modified
adult and family camp program was conducted at the former south side
location for several years, and in 1956 the improvements on this site
and the occupancy permit from the Forest Service were transferred to
the Episcopal Diocese of Olympia, which is rapidly developing a typical
church camp use and thereby carrying on the traditional purposes developed over 45 years by the YMCA.

The casualness with which one takes a two-hour drive from Portland over a fine, paved, forest road to Spirit Lake nowadays may cloud
the awareness of how relatively recent is this refinement. In the early
days of Y camping, boys went by boat down the Columbia River and up
the Cowlitz to Kelso, thence on to Castle Rock by train, wagon, stage or
laundry truck. Then they started hiking. Silver Lake would be the first
overnight stop; the second day would see them at the 18-mile board
(they called it Tipperary in those days); and the third day would have
them in camp. The return was equally simple!

Breaking camp and breakfasting soon after 3 a.m., campers would
be on the trail by 5:00 and would make camp at Joe Price's place atop
Green Mountain the first night. The second day would see them into
Castle Rock, where they took the train to Kelso, slept out on the station
lot overnight and boarded the Kellogg for Portland the next day. During
this era supplies went in by pack horse and wagon—supplies for the
season, that is. There was no running out to Castle Rock for fresh ice

cream for the evening meal. A Mrs. Lemmon had the contract for getting supplies to camp for some years, and driver Louis Pauley became a
great tradition with campers.

Rail transport to Castle Rock came along in 1916, and half a dozen
years later busses were used from Portland to the bottom of Green
Mountain, where hiking started. After the Coal Bank Road was improved and the road located on the north side of the Toutle to the lake,
modern bus transportation took boys to the lake shore and closed one of
the eras of camp history.

There is a kind of magic in the chemistry of a boy surrounded by
the clean, stark things of the natural world, discovering in companion-
ship with congenial friends and understanding adults the essential
truths about himself and the earth and God. A good many years ago an
old camper called Camp Meehan "the camp of enduring friendships."
During fifty years, alumni of Spirit Lake have grown to become leaders
in commerce and state. We like to believe their testimony when they
send their sons to camp, as hundreds of them have, that these enduring
friendships and the maturing experiences of camping on lake, trail and
mountain helped to shape the habits and outlook which have made
them effective citizens. And, we like to hope that the same experiences
happening to boys in 1959 will help produce leaders for Oregon's next
half century.

About 1912 at the Portland YMCA Camp. J.C. Meehan is pictured on the left.
Later the camp was named in his honor. Picture from the Lange/Whitney collection.

PART II

Very Early History

The Beginning

For those of us who are accustomed to crossing the Cowlitz River bridge at Castle Rock, a thought seldom comes to us that we are crossing an avenue of communication and commerce that is hundreds, and probably thousands, of years old.

This short quarter mile of channel stands alone in that it possesses an historic past. Upstream and downstream our restless meandering river has claimed, and then abandoned, a new course, only to appropriate another and then, perhaps, return to an old one.

For untold centuries before the "European Invasion," the Cowlitz Tribe of Native Americans pursued an extensive commerce in trade goods. The Cowlitz River was *their* highway. These tradesmen would pick up products of the Puget Sound tribes and those of the upper Cowlitz and swap them with the Chinooks of the lower Columbia, the Calapooias of Willamette Valley, and then with the numerous tribes of the upper Columbia. Occasionally they would go as far as Celilo Falls seeking trade goods from the far interior.

Without a doubt, white men paddled this river on many occasions before the 1800s. There is a map of the Cowlitz Valley that was supposedly drawn by a member of the Lewis and Clark Expedition (1804-06). There seems to be no documentation of this side trip, but the map would indicate a trip was made.

It is believed that the earliest *fully documented* story of a white man ascending our river is that of George Simpson, a factor of the Hudson's Bay Company. He made this trip in 1828 while inspecting company properties. He reported that the Cowlitz Tribe had several thousand members at that time. (They were nearly wiped out by white man's disease within the next few years.)

The Abbé Francois Norbet Blanchet, appointed by the Bishop of Quebec as Vicar General of the Oregon country, left Ft. Vancouver in

December of 1838 in a canoe paddled by Indians and arrived at the Cowlitz Prairie settlement on December 16, 1838, to celebrate the first Catholic Mass.

In 1838 the United States government sent Navy Lieutenant Charles Wilkes on an exploring trip in the Pacific. He reached the mouth of the Columbia in April 1841. After making extensive surveys in the Puget Sound area, he went to Cowlitz Prairie and made arrangements for two canoes to take the party down the Cowlitz and Columbia Rivers to Astoria. By the middle of June, Wilkes was in Vancouver, and on the 17th he sailed along the Columbia to the mouth of the Cowlitz. He then went up the Cowlitz River a short way but returned because of the very swift current.

On September 21, 1841, Wilkes went up the Cowlitz in his gig to finish the survey and "examine the strata of coal said to exist there." After ascending the river 13 miles, he turned back as "the water was so shallow, the boat would not float."

It was Wilkes who first charted the Toutle River under its present name. In 1853 the railroad surveyors showed the river as the "Sehquu" but the present name was restored in 1856.

James Gardiner

There are a few names that do not appear large in the history of our area but whose owners did play a part, in their way, and then just disappeared.

For a rather novel reason, James Gardiner is a small part of our story. James was born in Scotland, and we first hear of him in 1852 when he filed on a GDLC (Government Donation Land Claim) on the north bank of the Toutle River where it empties into the Cowlitz. Being a widower, with two sons, he was limited to 160 acres—actual acreage was 154.20.

This very early date of his filing placed him as the first white settler on the Toutle as well as the first in the vicinity of Castle Rock.

Gardiner established a hotel of sorts where boaters moving up or down the Cowlitz could get a meal and a place to sleep. He also served travelers of the old Hudson's Bay Trail. At this point they would have just forded the Toutle or were about to do so, depending on which way they were moving.

James was commonly known far and wide as "Hardbread" Gardiner as he invariably served that item with his meals. His will was proven in probate court September 14, 1858. The date of death was not stated.

Little else is known about this claim except that James' son, William A. Gardiner, was appointed administrator of the estate.

Should the question arise— "Who was the first settler in our area?"—we must again state that documentary evidence gives this honor to James Gardiner.

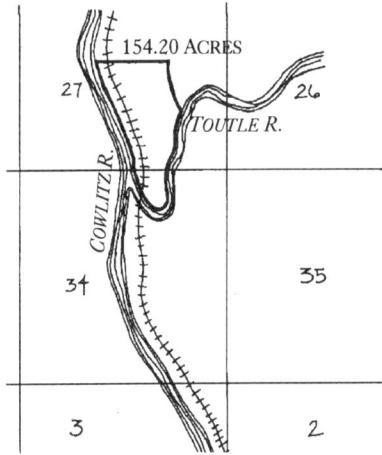

*1852 Plat of GDLC of
James (Hardbread) Gardiner*

County Road Bridge across the lower Toutle River, circa 1912

Tower—Settlements Along The Toutle River

by Pearl (nee Davidson) Woodard Blackwell

In 1882 Jacob and Olive Shafer with their six children left Nebraska by train for San Francisco, California. Then, by boat, they traveled to Portland, Oregon, where they crossed the Columbia River into Washington Territory.

Eventually they got to Toledo, Washington, where they bought 20 (writing unclear, 70?) acres of school land with a small house and a grove of large maple trees. Their first venture was to try making maple sugar from the sap, but it was a "no go." (There is a Section 16 School Land a couple of miles northeast of the present Tower bridge.)

The next year, 1883, the Shafers, Mrs. Shafer's parents, Mr. & Mrs. Joe Myers, a brother, Frank Myers, and two or three other families formed a settlement that was later called Tower.

The Shafers were evidently born to pioneer, as they had started pioneer homes in both Kansas and Nebraska. However, they had to

The first permanent Tower bridge, a suspension bridge over the Toutle River at Tower, built circa 1908

First Tower School, north of Poria home. This first school burned in a forest fire.

fight Indians so had moved, always west. In Washington they had no Indian troubles so decided to stay.

In 1886 they had their first school, taught by a Mr. Wilkerson in a room of his house, later District No. 35. Mr. Wilkerson was also postmaster at Tower, and Mr. Shafer had the contract for carrying mail between Toledo and Tower.

The community had its sorrows, and when two of the Shafer children died, they were buried in a small clearing over the hill from the Shafer house. It became the Tower Cemetery and there are about thirty graves there.

About five miles farther up the river was another settlement of about three families, each comprised of several children. In each neighborhood was a sprinkling of bachelor homesteaders. All of these people traded at Toledo, and the road was not much more than a cow trail.

About the same time, 1886, J.B. Poria, a brick and stone mason, arrived from Kansas. He had a wife and eight children. He bought the homestead right of a place two miles south of the Toutle River. There was a trail to Silver Lake, and five of his children went to what was called the Woodard School near Silver Lake. About the same time, four more families moved into the neighborhood. About 1890, School District No. 27 was formed. A log school house was built one mile north of the Poria home and children from three families attended the first

Second Tower School. It was located near the Tower Cemetery.

school. Among the first teachers was Charlie Rogers (a relative of the Congers of Castle Rock).

A road was built to Castle Rock and it became the trading center of this community. In 1891 J.L. Davidson moved to a homestead just north of the Toutle River and across the river from the Poria settlement. The Davidsons crossed the river by rowboats and traded at both Silver Lake and Castle Rock.

In late 1896 or early 1897 men from the Shafer settlement, three miles north of the Davidsons, and the men from the Poria settlement opened a road up the north side of the Toutle and built a bridge across the river at Davidsons, thus connecting all the settlements. (Note: This bridge was first known as the Manna Bridge and later as the Tower Bridge.)

The pioneers of those early Toutle settlements all started trading at Castle Rock. I haven't been able to learn why they stopped trading at Toledo unless the road down the river was less rugged than the one over the hills to Toledo.

All these early settlers raised gardens, put in orchards, and had cows and chickens. The men worked in shingle bolt camps and worked for the county, building and improving roads. At least four of these settlers were stone masons and worked at their trade when possible.

Mr. Poria often went to Portland to buy groceries and clothes for his large family. He traded at Jones Cash Store, and the story is told that he took along a string with knots tied along it for the various size shoes he must buy.

Tower Road construction—this road in its present location

Poria

by Leland Jackson

John Porier (French spelling) was born in St. Gregorier, Quebec, in 1847. Malvina Frichette was born in St. Dominic, Quebec, in 1849. They were married in Valley Falls, Rhode Island, in 1869. Six years and four children later, they were in Concordia, Kansas. While there, five more children were born.

In 1886 the family made a trip from Kansas to Castle Rock that took eight days. If their trip by Immigrant Train was typical of thousands of others, it was something like this:

The family was assigned one or two boxcars. One car was slightly and temporarily subdivided into areas that would serve as the kitchen, the "bathroom," the bedroom, or as needed. The second car, if present, would be loaded with household goods, tools, or supplies. The train moved in daylight hours only. As evening approached, the train was shunted onto a siding. The family then replenished the water supply, emptied the sanitary containers, cooked supper, prepared food for the next day, and then perhaps made their beds for the night. Early the next morning the train would be rolling again.

After arriving in Portland, Mr. Poria bought another man's homestead rights. The purchased land was near the present Tower Cemetery and is now about five miles from town. It was then nearer eight or nine miles from Castle Rock as the route was over the Schaffran Hill and down almost to the Carnine Road and then doubled back toward the Toutle River Valley and to their new home.

The Porias lived on their farm for 27 years. Three children were born there. The family was staunchly Roman Catholic. John was one of the prime movers in getting St. Mary's Church in Castle Rock built and furnished in 1903. He died in 1922.

The Storm Family

by Leland Jackson

Captain Hugo and Gisela Storm, a most interesting newlywed couple, settled in the Tower area in 1896. The groom was a retired Austrian sea captain. The bride was a talented string musician, also from Austria.

This story was lifted largely from an extensive article written by E.A. Underhill several years ago. The present writer was unable to determine the date or the newspaper from which the clippings were taken. Also, this story is much shorter:

At the age of twelve, Hugo Storm went to sea as an apprentice aboard a sailing ship. At the age of 27 he received his Master's papers and the command of his first ship, *The Mozart*. He lost this ship during a typhoon in the Bay of Kobi, Japan.

His second ship was *The Luebeck*, of which he was half owner. This interest was sold when he came to the United States in 1893.

His ports of call were all from Germany to the Orient and islands thereabouts—Bonner, Sumatra, Singapore, Dutch East Indies, and Formosa.

While in Singapore on one of his trips, he stayed at the Raffles Hotel where an orchestra of six sisters was entertaining the guests. One of the six sisters, Gisela, was invited to dine at Captain Storm's table. Unbeknownst to her, a romance was in the making.

The six sisters played as a unit of stringed instrumentalists. They were wined and dined by nobility in such countries as Russia, Germany and Egypt. An Italian count presented Gisela with a watch, which is now a family heirloom.

At that time and place it seems that it was a common practice for a man seeking the hand of a lady to propose to the parents before asking the young lady. Be that as it may, Captain Storm did just that. He wrote to Gisela's parents in Trieste.

Gisela knew nothing of this until she received an order to come home, pack her things, and leave for the United States. Her wishes seemingly were of no consideration. Whether there was a scene of protest over giving up her music career and an exciting life we do not know, but she did what she was told.

While she was preparing her trousseau, her older sister married a sea captain and moved to Hawaii. After two years, Gisela was ready with eleven trunks of dresses and linens. She arrived in Tacoma in 1896. Her sister from Hawaii came to the wedding.

Preceding all of this, the Captain had sent his mother and two brothers to take up a homestead in this area, preferably "near water."

After the wedding, the couple came to Toledo and traveled to their wilderness home by horseback. After being acclaimed by the nobility in Europe and other places, Mrs. Storm came to a log cabin in dense timber, with no near neighbors. Eleven trunks of feminine finery and dainty slippers that had graced the halls of conservatories of music had come to this. In 1898 lumber for a new home was carted in from Winlock over unbelievably rough roads. The new building with its glass fronted porch was large enough for the famous parties held there in later years.

People traveling in daylight only came by wagons, buggies, and horseback. Music was by local talent. The ladies slept in the house and the men made do in the barn or nearby shed.

It has been said that the basement was well stocked with beverages and the attic was a veritable museum of artifacts collected by the Captain on his many voyages.

Captain Storm died in 1927. Mrs. Storm lived in Castle Rock for several years. They were blessed with one child, Ella.

Note—The Conradi Still Meadow Farm now covers the Storm homestead.

Very Early Silver Lake

Early in the year of 1870 two men filed claims at Silver Lake. They were George White and James Farnsworth. Later in the year came David Germond, C. Caruthers, Charles Seaquest, P.M. Farnsworth, Captain George Pyle, A. Bullock, Andrew Dahlquist and wife, and the Tippery family.

Most of the first settlers filed on land close to the lake shore or along an old Indian trail that led to Yakima Valley.

Incidentally, Mr. Germond is credited with driving the first ox team from the Cowlitz River to Silver Lake.

John and Dora Wyant and their four daughters took a homestead at Toutle in 1875. The Boothe family located about a half mile west of the lake. The Carnine family also came about this time.

The Jacob Tippery Family

Official records and family tradition describe how Jacob Tippery emigrated from Alsace, now a part of France, to Maryland in the early 1700s. Our great-great-grandfather, Abraham Tippery (son of Jacob) was born in Maryland, March 26, 1788, and about this time the family moved to Sinking Valley, Pennsylvania, near Altoona, to work in the lead mines.

Abraham was mustered into the Militia for a six-month term during the War of 1812, serving at Erie, Pennsylvania. Afterward he hauled freight by wagon to and from central Pennsylvania to western Pennsylvania, a one-month trip. The principal cargo was flour and salt. Abraham's third son, Jacob, our great-grandfather, was born September 15, 1819. In the 1830s Abraham moved with his second wife, Catherine Harbst Tippery, and their younger children to Clarion County, Pennsylvania, where some of them worked at construction and maintenance on the Fox estate. Others farmed, worked in the iron furnaces, and pioneered in early Pennsylvania oil fields.

Jacob and his first wife, Mary Thompson Tippery, were the par-

ents of William, Miles, Harriet, Henrietta and Mary Ann. After his wife
Mary and baby Mary Ann died, Jacob and children lived for a while with
his elder brother William in Clarion County. About 1852 he married
Lucinda Willis Foster, who had been a housekeeper for his father's family. Following the deaths in infancy of their first two children, Jacob and
Lucinda and the four other children moved to Houston County, Minnesota, about 1856, together with brother William and family. Their oc-
cupations were farming and "river work" on the Mississippi. Sarah,
Mary Alice, Jacob, Effie and Ella May were born in Minnesota. William
and Miles served in the Minnesota Infantry during the Civil War, William dying in a Confederate prison.

The decision to immigrate to the West was made in 1869. They
traveled by ox team and covered wagon to Omaha, sold their outfit,
boarded one of the first trains to travel to San Francisco. They took passage there on the steamer *Ajax*, bound for Portland, Oregon. Lucinda
and the younger children lived in a small house near the site of the
Morrison Street bridge for about eight months while Jacob and son
Miles sought a new home site. February 13, 1870, Jacob wrote to his
daughter Henrietta at Montevideo, Minnesota, as follows:

Dear Daughter,

We are all well. Hoping this may find you as it leaves
me. We are living in Portland, Oregon. I have not found
Washington to be what I expected. There is very little good
farming land in it, not enough to make a farming country.
Lumbering will be the principal business. I have been
through a good part of it. I don't want any of it. Oregon is
good enough for any person—good rich soil as there is any
place, but it is all taken here. I am going off southeast of this
near the state line. George Gray of Lansing says there is
plenty of government land there and is a better climate
(than) there is in this part of the state. I am going there next
week. We have very fine weather here. The ground has not
froze this winter and there had not been snow but plenty of rain.

Grass is green, peach trees are in bloom. This is the
best place for fruit of all kinds I ever seen—apples, fifty cts.

per bushel, pears, 1.00 per bushel, flour, 2 and 2.50 per hundred, potato .50 per bushel, smoked meat shoulder 10, side 15, ham 16 cts. per pound. Cows $30 to $40 per head. Sheep 1.50 a head. Horses from 25 to 200 per head. Wheat .65 to .75 per bushel. Cows live here all winter without feed and keep in good order.

This is a large city, eight thousand inhabitants. It is on the Willamet River twelve miles from the Columbia. Ocean ships all come here and get loads of flour and meat, apples, oats, and barley. Last week the steam ship *Moses Taylor* took seven thousand dozen of eggs at one time down to Frisco.

I like this very well and would like it much better if I was on a good farm. A free passage would not get me back to Minn. Everything in the clothing line is cheaper than in Minn. Our passage from Winnebago Valley was $433 dollars.

My best respects to all,

—Jacob Tippery

After months of seeking, their choice was a homestead at the end of Silver Lake, the easterly part. The family then journeyed down the Columbia by steamer to Monticello, then on up the Cowlitz by rowboat to Castle Rock. They lived in a house on the Jackson place on the west side of the river while Jacob and Miles built a log house with a stick and mud fireplace on the homestead. Moving to the new home, they walked the eight-mile blazed Indian trail through thick old-growth forest. Mother and baby Ella May rode horseback.

They lived by hunting, trapping, and fishing. Jacob often worked away from home. Land was laboriously cleared of timber and brush, fruit trees planted, a garden space cleared. In the fall of 1871, Minnie, their last child, was born. Jacob's elder daughter Harriet and her husband, William Morrill, moved from Minnesota to a place close by. On March 31, 1872, Jacob wrote again to Henrietta:

Dear Daughter,

We are all well except myself. I have a sore come under my arm which has stopped me from work for some days, and

I don't know how it will terminate yet, but think I will have to get it cut out before it will get well. I received yours of Jan. 7 in March. I thought you had forgotten your friends out here. We all wrote letters but got no answers.

We live 65 miles from Portland by the river and 25 from the Columbia and 6 miles from the North Pacific Railroad. We can hear the cars running here at home. There is 25 miles in running order and they are to work on the next 60 which is to be finished by fall. This runs from the Columbia River to the Sound.

We have very fine weather here. The leaves are beginning to come out. I have got lots of cherry, plum and pear trees that I planted last spring. Some are coming out in bloom now. I expect they will have some fruit this year. I have got one hundred trees planted. When this (rail) road is finished you can come out and get all the fruit you want. We have eleven cows. The wolves killed three calves for me and four for Morrill. I killed one wolf last somer but we will give some of them a dose some of these days.

You wanted to know how we liked that gun I got of Mason. It is not good but I knock a deer endways when I hit him. I don't hunt much. There is plenty of bear, deer, panther and wolves and some lynx. I understand you got nearly burnt out last fall. I wish you had some of the cedar timber that is here to rebuild your fences. I can split rails 40 feet long.

We are going to plant our potatoes this week. I sowed onion seed two weeks ago. We don't have no winter here. We had a little snow this winter; it laid on six days. Our coldest weather is about like yours in October.

This is hard country to make a farm in—it is nearly all brush or timber land. There is some small prairies but they are spread on very thin, but the brush land is very good. Timber land is not so good.

Good tame grass, vegetables and fruit—the world cannot beat it! We had a mess of letice and radish this week.

We don't feed cattle much here; they run out in the woods all winter. Sometimes they will eat hay but not often.

Flour 1.43 per hundred, coffee 25 cts., shugar 11 cts., bacon 16 cts. potatoes 1.00 per B, syrup, best, 1.00 per gallon. Wages are very good, 1.50 per day and board, in gold. They don't use paper here. It is all gold and silver.

I lost another calf the night before Easter. I found it all covered up. I put some strychnine on it and the next morning I found a mountain lion laying dead. He was seven feet long. He weigh two hundred pounds. This is eight calves he killed, four for me and four for Morrill. I skinned it and stuffed its hide. I think of starting a menagerie.

Jacob died of his injury in a hospital in Vancouver in 1872. (He is buried in the Silver Lake Cemetery.) Mary Alice married John Martin, Jacob Jr. married Emma Carnine, Ella May married Charles Carnine, Minnie married Thomas Carnine, Effie married Judd Bemis. Miles Tippery married Eunice Gilmore and Sarah Ann married Mario Monohon. For this double wedding the brides had made their gowns, also their hats.

Left with six children to care for, Lucinda raised garden produce, pigs and cattle. Miles, the only adult male, trapped, hunted, and cut shingle bolts to float down the tortuous Toutle River. Lucinda managed to have a large house built, reminiscent, it is said, of a Pennsylvania farmhouse.

Eastern relatives read an account in a newspaper of the celebration of the golden wedding anniversaries of the Carnine-Tippery couples. They had heard that the Tippery family had been eaten by bears after they left Pennsylvania. (Submitted by Miles W. Tippery and Mrs. Beth Buzzard)

The Miles Tippery & Will Tippery Familes

by Miles W. Tippery

My grandfather, Miles Tippery, a pioneer homesteader in the Silver Lake/Toutle District, was born November 16, 1843, in Blair County, Pennsylvania, the second child of Jacob and Mary Thompson Tippery.

About 1856 the family moved to Winnebago Valley, Houston County, Minnesota, near the Mississippi River. There, as a teenager, Miles worked at farming, cutting ice for storage, harvesting wild rice Indian fashion, trapping muskrats, loading river boats, and catching cat fish for market—learning many skills he would later use in Washington Territory.

During the Civil War he enlisted in Company K, 11th regiment, Minnesota Infantry, and served in Tennessee. After the war he worked at railroad construction, and then in 1869 traveled with his family to homestead in the Northwest—(See "The Jacob Tippery Family.") Miles' homestead was situated just west of the present Toutle Lake School, the N.E. 1/4 Section 25, Twp. 10 N., Range 1 W.W.M.

In the summer he cut shingle bolts and then drove them down the Toutle in the fall. He started trapping at Silver Lake, using an Indian dugout canoe. Soon he built a log cabin at Spirit Lake and began trapping more valuable furs—marten, fisher, lynx. In November he would hire a teamster to haul in supplies and food to last all winter. He and his partner worked their trap lines on snow shoes, often staying out overnight in lean-to shelters. About April 1 the wagon would return to haul out their furs.

One morning their dog treed a cougar. When Miles aimed his rifle, his partner, Elmer Gilmore, asked to shoot it, as he had never killed a cougar. Elmer fired and the cougar fell to the snow. Miles seized the 150 pound cat by the base of the tail and held it up. Only stunned by a head wound, it revived and began to bite and claw him. Sixty-five years later Elmer told me, "I couldn't shoot for fear of hitting your grandfather, so I picked up a big limb and started clubbing the cougar, which soon let go of him and ran off."

Later, Miles and his brother-in-law, John Martin, built and operated a water-powered saw mill on the outlet of Silver Lake near the present Community Church.

Miles' wife, Eunice Gilmore Tippery, was born June 4, 1869, at Dutch Flat, California. She was the daughter of Lyman W. Gilmore— who traveled from Maine to California in a sail ship via Cape Horn in 1852 to work in the gold fields—and his wife Sarah who made the voyage in 1860. The Gilmore family later moved to the Toutle district.

Miles and Eunice agreed with Osgood Bullock, an older Civil War veteran who had a homestead on Hemlock Creek in the Slightly district, that if Miles would help build a new house and Eunice provide housekeeping and old-age care for Bullock, they could live there and inherit the property upon his death. Built about 1890, the house included a fireplace made of pumice quarried at the outlet of the lake.

Their daughter, Mabel Gertrude, was born July 14, 1889, and son, Will Arthur, born March 31, 1891. After the death of Eunice November 15, 1893, Bullock made another housekeeping arrangement and sold Miles the south forty acres of his property. Miles built a small house there in the early 1890s and cleared 15 acres of creek bottom land. A larger house, built in the early 1900s, remained the family residence until destroyed by fire in 1946. Miles continued his lonely trapping work which necessitated boarding Mabel and Will with neighbors and relatives much of the year.

Mable and her husband, Albert E. Hayer, raised six children in California.

Will married Ethel L. Cook, daughter of David M. and Frances R. Cook who moved from Kansas to Oregon and then to Lewis County where Ethel was born September 27, 1890, at Centralia. She taught at several rural schools, including Sightly. They lived with Miles and gradually developed a small dairy while Will worked in the timber industry. Their children are Miles W., Chesley D., Betty E. (Mrs. Fred Brown), Bernita E. (Mrs. William Kessler), Mabel F. (Mrs. Andrew Carasco), and Richard L.

Miles remained active around the farm until the early 1920s. When a bear raided the pasture and carried a hog into the forest, he trapped it. The warm, black fur was our best rug for many years. At age

80 he was working alone, hewing timbers with a broad axe for a new barn, when the axe slipped and deeply cut his foot. He nearly bled to death but managed to hobble 500 feet to the house where Ethel stopped the bleeding until Dr. Quaife arrived hours later. He never could walk well afterward but still enjoyed fishing. Miles died July 21, 1929, and was buried with military honors at Silver Lake Cemetery.

Our big event was the trip to Castle Rock about once a month. The "county road" to our place was impassable for cars, so we traveled six miles in the rowboat down Hemlock Creek and across Silver Lake to Barnes' store and caught the "stage," and then returned home in the evening. Always difficult, the trip was dangerous in the storms, fog and early darkness of winter. Not until 1930 did we have a gravel road.

Will suffered severe injuries when he fell from a building in 1931. During his long hospitalization and recovery, Miles, 14, and Chesley, 12, operated the farm while attending school. Betty, Bernita and Mabel began housework early and later assisted with farming. Ethel canned up to one thousand quarts of food per year besides the many other difficult tasks of raising a family in rather primitive conditions. Unable to continue in the woods, Will changed to sales work and beef cattle. The family home is presently operated as a cattle ranch by Richard Tippery.

The R. S. Carnine Family

(Original letter by Beth Buzzard)

(The following reprints of the Tippery and Carnine families were taken from pages 179-310 of *The History Of Cowlitz County, Washington*—circa 1983 Cowlitz County Historical Society.)

The first records of the Carnine family disclose that one Phillipse Leendert Conyn (later became Carnine) immigrated to America from Holland in 1640. The family had descended from French Huguenots, fleeing to Holland in the 16th century. Phillipse's name was found on church records at Beaverwyck, New York, dated about 1655.

The journey of the Carnine family from the east to west coasts was marked by settlements at Boundbrook, New Jersey, and then the Conewage settlement in Pennsylvania (about 1765). Further emigrations led down the Ohio River to Harrodsburg, Kentucky, where they helped found "The Old Mud Meeting House." The restless trail led across the continent to Indiana, Missouri, Kansas, and finally Cowlitz County in Washington Territory. Richard Seth Carnine was born in Ripley County, Indiana, July 10, 1841, to Lydia and Allen Carnine. Came 1861, Richard enlisted in the Union Army and served for two years. St. Louis, Missouri, was where he met his wife-to-be, Hanna (Kate) Smith, born in Kentucky. They married December 15, 1863. They lived in Missouri for several years, moving to Kansas in 1868. Wild prairie country it was. Emma, their first child, was born in Missouri. They lived at first in a sod house. One morning Richard and Katy arose to survey the damage done to their crops by a horde of grasshoppers.

"We'll never plant another seed in Kansas, Katy," said Richard. Plans were soon formulated to go west. Many friends and relatives gathered that last day of May, 1875, to bid goodbye. There were four Carnine children by this time—Tom, Charles, Emma (Tippery) and Myrtle, the baby. Richard was captain of the wagon train. The journey, 2000 miles to the west, was long and arduous, saddened by the sudden death of little Myrtle in western Idaho. How difficult it was to go on the next day, leaving the little grave behind! They proceeded to the Dalles, taking a steamer down the Columbia to Vancouver. They remained there while Richard sought a suitable spot to locate. They eventually settled on a homestead at the west end of Silver Lake. The house Great-grandfather Richard built remains today, occupied by a descendant of the family.

This was in 1876. A school was built by the Carnine family and neighbors. Teachers at one time or another in this school were Mrs. Pyle, Mrs. Marie Hun-

Large home near Silver Lake—possibly Mangs home. Note puncheon road in front.

tington, Miss Jeanie Whittle, Miss Anna Patton, and J. G. Bruce.

Carnine children born in Washington Territory were Maude (Graham), Lulu (Wells), Milo, and Edgar (Ned).

The Carnines were far-mers—raised enough stock for their own use with some to sell or trade in Portland, the trading center. They traveled there by boat now and then. Many descen-dants of the Carnine and

Charles Carnine, Earl Carnine, Richard Setch Carnine (a Civil War veteran), Richard Carnine

Tippery family live in Cowlitz County and other places in Washington, Oregon and Hawaii.

Mangs Family Tree Has Gardner Branches

by Mrs. Ray Slack

TOUTLE—Mary Victoria Wickman was born in Uleaborg, Finland, November 5, 1862. She came to America at the age of 24, living with her brother Fred until her marriage in Astoria to John Mangs on July 29, 1888.

John Mangs was born in Laphyard, Finland, April 10, 1849. He came to Astoria while still a young man, fishing on the Columbia River for several years, also taking a homestead claim at Silver Lake. Seven years later, he, his wife and two daughters, Mary Hannah and Alida Victoria, moved onto the place where twins, Bessie and Bertha, a son, Fred Stephen, and another daughter, Elizabeth Lena, were added to the family group.

Fred now operates the old homestead, raising a few beef cattle, also some hay and timber.

Mary Miner lives on the adjoining place, northeast of the old homestead. Alida married Joe Gardner, and Bertha married Harry Gardner, both of Toutle. Bessie was married to Pleasant Francisco, and they were living on the Walburg place across the lake from the homestead when she passed away in 1918.

Elizabeth married John Jokela of Centralia. He died in 1927. She lives on the homestead by her brother Fred.

There were 12 grandchildren, 2 of whom have died, and 25 greatgrandchildren.

John Mangs died at his home at Silver Lake in 1912. Mary Mangs died in 1937 at the home place. Both are buried in the Silver Lake Cemetery.

Silver Lake Schools

This material was taken from some old notes of Mellie Lee Davis Jackson and is believed to be from information given to her by Mrs. Tom Carnine.

The first school at Silver Lake was on the Hiram Germond homestead. In 1876 an abandoned log house was repaired so that school could be held in it. Matilda Huntington was the first teacher. School was held here for but a short time, as the building became infested with bed bugs and the children were moved to another log house that had been repaired by the neighbors.

The next school was a log house built by the neighbors on an acre of ground given to the district by Richard Carnine. Money was subscribed for buying windows and furniture. Each district at that time was supposed to have three months of school, but a Mr. Peters who was interested in schools donated work on the building, helped to get money for an extra three months, and taught. He organized debating teams, spelling bees, sings and other entertainments for the settlers. He then went to Arkansas and did the same thing for those people.

Later, a school was built where the Grange Hall is now. This location was used until the Toutle Lake School was organized. Among the early teachers were Emma Tippery, Sarah Pyle, Francis Marion Woodard, and, of course, Matilda Huntington and Mr. Peters, previously mentioned in this article.

(Sarah Pyle was the first *district* school teacher (i.e., supported by public tax dollars). Her husband, Captain Pyle, came after the Civil War and homesteaded in the vicinity of Succor Creek. Later, when Sarah Pyle was the Silver Lake District schoolteacher, she rowed back and forth across Silver Lake to school every day.)

Woodard

Francis Marion Woodard was an interesting and capable person who came to the Silver Lake area in the 1880s. He was a graduate of Valparaiso College in Valparaiso, Indiana.

In 1882 Mr. Woodard filed on a homestead near what is now the junction of the Schaffran and Gibson Roads. In his earlier days he had worked in a cooperage and had become proficient with woodworking tools. It was said of him that if a needed item was made of wood he could make it.

When his split-log, two-story house was finished, he brought his wife and four children from Portland where they had been staying.

Silver Lake School of 1889. This school was often called the Woodard School. It was located near the intersection of Paine Road and Stankey Road.

The Woodard homestead near Silver Lake. The house burned in a 1918 forest fire.

As one would expect, Woodard was soon hired as a school teacher. He taught for some years at the Silver Lake School on the Paine Road. For a quite obvious reason, it was frequently referred to as the Woodard School.

A short note in *The Advocate*, dated August 12, 1898, states that F.M Woodard was attending the Teachers' Institute in Kalama.

Green River Bridge

The Advocate, February 4, 1897:

"Victor Carlson, of the upper Toutle country, was in town last Thursday and Friday. He informed us that he and other residents of his road district have built the piers and placed the stringers of a bridge built across Green River this winter. Some iron bolts are yet required to brace the stringers before the bridge is ready for covering. The energy of the Toutle people is truly commendable."

Francisco Stage

In the summer of 1915, it was my good fortune to ride on a stage that was truly one of a kind. This motor vehicle made regular trips between Toutle and Castle Rock.

Pleasant Francisco, a genius with tools, took a Gram Bernstein chassis, a Ford radiator, and other diverse parts and developed a four-seated conveyance that did the intended job surprisingly well.

It had hard rubber tires that accurately counted each and every bump on the road.

There was a flat top but no doors or side curtains. At the time I rode on it, there was no windshield. The ride was not a stuffy one, be assured!

Francisco Stage

Frank G. Barnes & Silver Lake, Washington

Frank Grant Barnes was born in Gentry County, Missouri, in 1868, to a Civil War veteran from New York State. His farming family moved to Humboldt County, California, in 1881. Frank attended school in Missouri and California. He completed his education at Eureka (California) Academy and Business College.

Barnes came to Washington in 1891, and after looking around,

Looking south from the top of a water tower at the Barnes and Bull Mill. The Barnes store is the closest building. The school is in the dim top left corner. It was located where the Silver Lake Grange Hall now stands. The Grange Hall was once the school gymnasium.

The Silver Lake School House

settled at Silver Lake, which was to be his home for the next 30 years. He married Eleanora Dahlman of Silver Lake in 1893. The bride was the daughter of early-day immigrant settlers from Sweden. Frank and Eleanora were to have five children.

We next read of him as being engaged in the shingle and lumber business in a partnership with Frank Bull, a former neighbor in California. Bull died in 1898. Barnes succeeded him as the postmaster and apparently took over the Bull business interests as well.

In time Frank acquired much property and operated the mills and a large store successfully for the next two decades. He owned most of the town and the many rough board houses that lined the main street that is now a section of the Spirit Lake Memorial Highway.

The Silver Lake Railway & Lumber Company

In 1902 Mr. Barnes, E.S. Collins, J.A. Byerly and E.W. Ross incorporated the Silver Lake Railway and Lumber Company as a common carrier. Barnes was the cooperate secretary.

The logging operations of the Silver Lake Railway and Lumber Company was the economic mainstay of the Silver Lake area for many years. Their first logging operations were in the vicinity of what is now

The Barnes and Bull Mill, Silver Lake Road. Note the puncheon road.

The F.G. Barnes home at Silver Lake

The Barnes' store at Silver Lake. A ballroom was upstairs.

The Barnes and Bull Mill

the junction of the Memorial Highway and the South Silver Lake Road. The headquarters camp was known as Springtown. It was located at the point where Spring Creek joins Salmon Creek. The logging train hauled the logs from this operation to a pocket boom on the Cowlitz River about a mile south of Castle Rock.

The local nickname for the railroad was The Punkin Vine, as the roadbed followed the Salmon Creek with its many kinks throughout its length. The many steep grades and the handset brakes made railroading a very hazardous occupation.

In the 1920s, when most of the timber on the north side of the lake was logged off, the logging operation was sold to the Ostrander Railway and Timber Company, and the Silver Lake Railway and Lumber Company went out of existence. The rail lines were abandoned.

In 1924 Frank Barnes sold his interests in the logging company and had already moved his shingle mill to Kalama. He then moved to what is now Longview, where he had acquired some 700 acres of land. He later sold this to the R.A. Long Company as a site for a city. Mr. Barnes served as a state senator for Cowlitz County for many years.In 1902 the Silver Lake Railway and Lumber Company was incorporated as a Common Carrier. (A Common Carrier has the Right of Eminent Domain and thus can force the unwilling land owner to sell or grant a right-of-way. This railroad was obligated to accept and haul freight for others.)

The incorporators were Frank G. Barnes, E.S. Collins, F.A. Byerly, and E.W. Ross. The railroad was built to transport logs from the Silver

The Springtown cook house of the Silver Lake RR & Lumber Company

Lake area to the Cowlitz River. The pocket boom, "dump," was about a mile south of Castle Rock.

This new railroad, commonly referred to as The Punkin Vine, followed the crooked Salmon Creek as far as the present South Silver Lake Road and then into the Silver Lake basin, with branches in all directions. The line was ultimately to reach almost to the Coal Bank bridge on the Spirit Lake Memorial Highway.

After many years of operation, the line was abandoned, and the Charlie R. McCormick Lumber Company rebuilt the Salmon Creek section and extended it into the Tower area.

The Silver Lake logging operations were sold to the Ostrander Railway and Lumber Company. The logs were then hauled to the mill at Ostrander or boomed in the Cowlitz River at the mouth of Ostrander Creek.

There is still a logging railway into the Toutle area. It is operated by the Weyerhaeuser Company as a mainline operation. Truck roads feed the logs to the rail heads.

Planked bridge, Silver Lake. The east end of this bridge goes to the George Taylor Road, near the Silver Lake Cemetery. It was abandoned in the early 1930s. The pilings can still be seen. Photo from the Lange/Whitney collection.

Model T on the way to Spirit Lake

The logging operations of this area and the technical developments have been much the same as those in other areas of the Pacific Northwest.

First Settlers Of Toutle Area Found River To Be Both Obstacle & Source Of Livelihood

by Anabel E. Conradi

Though the ever-changing Toutle River on its frantic rush to the Cowlitz was often an obstacle, it was also of inestimable benefit to early settlers in that area, providing them with food and a means of livelihood.

The Toutle country in the early days began a little above Silver Lake and roughly comprised Toutle proper—site of Toutle post office, school and store; Sightly; Tower; Green Mountain; Kid Valley; and later extending to Lithow and St. Helens.

Homesteaders were late in arriving in the Toutle country as compared with Freeport, Castle Rock and even Silver Lake. The Whittles and the Jacob Tipperys were among the first to arrive at Silver Lake. But it was in 1876 before John Wyant came to the Toutle, followed soon by Newt Beighle, C.H. Horning and Henry Powelson. The Gilmores, Hallecks, bachelor Bullock, and later, the Moores, were among the first in the Sightly area.

(Correction: Although William Whittle built the first sawmill at Silver Lake and established the first store, he never settled there as he had already lived on a GDLC west of Castle Rock since 1855.)

1882 & 1889 Immigrations

The year 1882, however, saw a heavy immigration—a steady stream of settlers arrived that year to file on homesteads in the Toutle, Sightly and Green Mountain areas. Among those arriving in 1882 were the families of Joseph Price and Napoleon Bonaparte Gardner (known to one and all as N.B. or "Pole".) The Gardners played a very important part in the development of the Toutle area.

More settlers continued to arrive, but it was not until 1889 that another heavy immigration took place. Once a family was settled, it seems they could not wait to write their relatives and friends and urge them to come out.

Some of the early settlers were Mangs, Rogers, Hoffstadt, Pauley, Edward, Lafferty, White, Feist, Reiman, Le Gault, Searles, Bohn, P. Ferguson, Conradi, Umiker, Chism, Swanson, Finkas and Benson.

Early settlers at the mouth of the Green River were Pete Olson and Louie Peterson. Early settlers at Tower were Ben Beighle, Adolph Ritter, James Wilkinson, Jacob Shafer, the Lockes, John and Frank Storm and their mother, Walters, Davidsons, and the Williams family.

Rugged Conditions

By the 1870s, civilization was beginning to arrive along the Cowlitz. The settlers who penetrated into the Toutle country faced the most primitive conditions and forests as dense as any in the United States.

It seems that everyone, whether arriving by buckboard, wagon, horseback or on foot, arrived in a cold, driving rain. Many must have felt as little Foster Gardner did, who huddled shivering and forlorn in the wagon and said to his father, "What did we come out here for anyway?" At first sight of the desolate wilderness to which they had come, many of the women cried—others took it more cheerfully. But even those who cried soon wiped the tears away—there was too much to do to spend time weeping.

Almost everyone homesteaded at first. Some were lucky enough to buy relinquished rights from some discouraged homesteader and so had at least a shelter into which to move, but most did not. Clearing even a garden patch was a Herculean task, due to the size of the timber and the obstacles under which they worked—for instance, the lack of blasting powder.

Long Hard Winters

Many of the early arrivals got here in the late fall, facing a long hard winter with only the barest necessities for food. No milk, eggs, butter, fruit or vegetables. Once the ground was under cultivation the crops were amazing. There were no bugs, insects or worms to complicate things. Rutabagas weighing up to 35 pounds and turnips up to 15 pounds, yet sweet and juicy, were common. Seven potatoes, standing upright and coming to the top, filled a square, five-gallon oil can.

Fish and wild game provided most of the food, the women often doing the fishing and in a half hour's time coming home with all the 18 to 20 inch trout they could carry.

Industry Lifesaver

The shingle bolt industry was rapidly getting underway along the Cowlitz, and soon the Toutle settlers were cutting shingle bolts and floating them down the river to the booms at Castle Rock and Kelso. It took rugged, hardy men to get these bolts into and down the river before the high water came, and jams were frequent.

Jim Price says it took as many as 65 days sometimes to make a drive. Lacking mules or oxen, men have been known to buck them as much as a mile to the river.

The shingle bolt industry proved a lifesaver to those settlers, providing them with extra money from a crop already on their lands ready to harvest, with the river conveniently providing them with transportation for their product.

There were no roads to start with, only trails. No bridges either. Fording places were scarce as the river was larger and swifter than now. The huge trees lining the banks were felled for footlog crossings but were usually swept away in the high waters. In about 1890 Charles Conradi carried his kitchen stove on his back across a footlog to his homestead across the river. He had carried it that way all the way from Gardner's store, dragging a hand sled loaded with other supplies at the same time.

In the 1890s the development of the copper mines at Spirit Lake began. This provided additional employment for the settlers, both by working in the mines and by hauling supplies from Castle Rock to the mines—at first by pack trains and later by wagon.

Soon the settlers acquired cattle which ran wild through the woods and swamps. At that time there was lush grass and wild hay growing along the mountain slopes, and the cattle thrived.

Homes Deserted

Due to the lack of bridges, adequate roads, and transportation facilities, many of the original settlers sold out and moved away. Deserted homesteads by the dozens are to be found along Green Mountain, on up above Toutle and on the abandoned road above Tower. Later, the development of the logging industry in this area brought roads and bridges.

Schools Established

The heavy immigration of 1882 brought a need for schools, and on November 20, 1882, School District No. 30, known as Toutle River School, was established. The first school was held in 1883 with an enrollment of 21. I.R. Edwards was the teacher. Two years later the school at Sightly was organized. The Tower School came in 1886, the Kid Valley School in 1889, the Green Mountain School in about 1897, and the Conradi School about the same time.

The Conradi School is still standing on the old Conradi place, which is bisected by the new Toledo cut-off road from Spirit Lake Highway. The last school built at Toutle before they moved the location to its present site still stands on property owned by Joe Gardner. It is a large, yellow, frame building built in 1912 and was modern for its day.

Church services were held in the school houses but many times prior to that in private homes.

Post Offices Established

The Toutle Post Office was established in 1883, with Pole Gardner as postmaster. Paul Johnson was the first mail carrier and carried the mail on his back from Castle Rock. The Sightly Post Office was established at about the same time. The post office at Toutle remained in the Gardner name for 64 years. The Hallecks took care of the mail at Sightly in the early days.

Jim Eaton, brother-in-law of Jim Price and grandfather of George Eaton of Castle Rock, also used to carry the mail on foot. He lived above Gardners and needed a new floor for his cabin. So, on his way from Castle Rock, he used to stop at Johnny Martin's mill at the outlet of the lake and get one board of rough lumber and carry it, in addition to his mail sack, all the way up to his cabin.

Jim Price carried mail on horseback to Toutle and Sightly, staying overnight in Castle Rock at Uncle Bill Huntington's place and returning the next day to Toutle and Sightly.

Jim Wilkinson had the first post office at Tower and brought the mail from Winlock on horseback. The old Military Road from Winlock used to run at the top of the ridge back of the old Storm house. Tower Road used to continue on and up over the famous "Harvel Hill" and was the main road to Green River and St. Helens. The Tower postmasters used to carry the mail from Tower on up to Lithow on the Green River and later to St. Helens and Pauly. Two of the old Tower post offices are still standing on the former Storm and Williams places.

Celebrations Marked

With rivers to ford and only trails to ride, social life was hard won. But, there was always a big picnic on special holidays like the Fourth of July, with everyone coming from far and wide.

Dances were held at one of the larger homes or at the school houses and were always all-night affairs. Girls came on horseback— riding through the dark woods over steep hills and down spooky, black canyons for a bit of gaiety. They wore divided skirts and carried their party dresses and high-heeled slippers tied on behind their saddles.

Where once were Indian trails and rutted wagon roads, there are paved roads, extending all the way to beautiful Spirit Lake.

Lumbering is the chief industry, but the area is best known as a vacation spot. There are many parks along the sparkling Toutle River where vacationers can come for picnicking, swimming, fishing, camping, or to just enjoy the scenery.

(Note—It should be understood that many of the very early settlers arrived from the Toledo area instead of the Castle Rock area. This was because there was no bridge across the Toutle River until later, while there was a road (of sorts) from Toledo into the Toutle country.— *Longview Daily News, Cowlitz-Columbia Centennial Edition*)

Napoleon Boneparte Gardner
Brought Family To Toutle River Area In 1882

by Anabel E. Conradi

Probably no one family or person exerted the influence on the development of the Toutle area as did the Gardners, headed by the beloved and respected Napoleon Bonaparte Gardner, known to one and all as "N.B." or "Pole".

Pole and his wife, Nellie Ada Lapham Gardner, and their three children—Hiram, Foster and Fanny—arrived at Toutle in November 1882. He had been a surveyor, lawyer and prosecuting attorney back in Kansas. The family had first lived at Baldwin, Kansas, and then later at the town of Lawrence. Pole freighted from Lawrence to New Mexico, and then returned to Kansas for his family. While Mrs. Gardner was living in Lawrence, the town was visited by Quantros' raiders and burned. Pole left with his family and with a load of freight for New Mexico again and then on to San Francisco.

They came to Portland from San Francisco by boat and then on to Castle Rock. Newt Beighle, already settled on the Toutle, was a brother-in-law to Pole, and it was his enthusiasm about this country that had brought them. It took two days to make the trip from Castle Rock out to the Toutle country. They stopped overnight at the original Ben Beighle cabin. The evening of the second day, while attempting to climb a very steep hill (the one up to the present Varner ranch), they became so mired in the mud they could proceed neither forward nor backward. As usual there was a cold bitter rain falling and they became very discouraged.

Decision Reversed

It was then that the cheery voice of Newt Beighle was heard, and he took them to the shelter and warmth of his cabin for the night. The next morning they were determined to leave the Toutle country, and, after extricating their wagon, they headed back toward Castle Rock. Fortunately for the Toutle people, they met Henry Powelson on his way to sell the relinquishment rights to his homestead, and Pole promptly bought them and moved his family in.

Almost immediately he started the Toutle store and a blacksmith shop. Their home became an overnight stop, and the Gardner settlement became the hub around which the Toutle country revolved. It was sort of a community gathering place. Gardner was engaged in a number of different things and provided considerable employment to other settlers.

In 1883 the Toutle Post Office was organized with Pole as postmaster and the Toutle School was established. For 64 years the Toutle Post Office was in the Gardner name. Toutle soon became a thriving little community. It was located then, as now, just across the South Toutle River bridge. By the 1890s, there were over 100 persons in the South Toutle area.

Disaster Strikes

And then disaster stuck! A sudden flood took out the booms at Castle Rock and Kelso, and every shingle bolt in the Cowlitz and Columbia was swept out to sea. Pole had extended credit to the shingle bolt men and had purchased some of the shingle bolts outright. He owed the wholesaler in Portland $10,000. He went to see the wholesaler, told him he could not pay him, and asked him to come to Toutle and take over his assets. Mr. Lewis, the wholesaler, had faith in Pole's integrity and refused to do so.

It was then that Avery Gilmore, a bachelor from Sightly, drew his $800 in savings from the bank and brought it to Pole Gardner. "Take it," he said, "and use it for three things only to be doled out to those in the direst need; pay me back when you can." The three things were flour, beans and bacon. The money was spent for nothing else, and these items were given sparingly to those whose need was the greatest. It became Pole's lifetime work, says his son Joe, paying back that $10,000.

Many Destitute

Harry Gardner, son of Pole, says about that winter: "Many of the settlers were left destitute to face the oncoming winter. Often I have seen men come into the only store in the valley to see if possibly something had turned up that would give them a few days' work. Then, slipping out back of the building they would drag out of their pocket a hunk of cold, boiled, blue, winter-killed venison with perhaps a scrawny, cold, boiled potato for their lunch. Then, they would have to go home to families who would have to subsist a while longer on this meager fare. Had it not been for the kindness of Avery Gilmore, this country would have been much more retarded in its settlement."

Five other children were born to the Gardners—Bird, Ada, N.B., Harry and Joe. Pole's three brothers—Len, Dave and Bill—also came to the Toutle later on, and all took up homesteads.

The Laphams also came out as a result of the Gardners' urging, as Mrs. Gardner was born a Lapham. Mrs. Gardner was a very talented person, writing many poems and hymns. One of her most beautiful and better-known hymns is *Heaven Is Over All*. Pole died in 1918 and Mrs. Gardner in 1938.

Harry Gardner ran the old store for a while, and then Foster Gardner did. But it was finally discontinued. Later, Harry ran a store and filling station, but it too was discontinued when Depression days came. The Gardners and other Toutle residents fought bitterly against changing the Spirit Lake Road, which used to run right by Toutle and on up to Green Mountain, but it was to no avail.

Mangs Arive

from "The Advocate", August 13, 1953:

The John Mangs family came to Silver Lake in 1885, and two of the Mangs girls, Bertha and Alida, married Harry and Joe Gardner. Three other Mangs children are still living—Fred Mangs of Silver Lake and Lizzie and Mary.

Harry lives on the original Pole Gardner place and is logging and ranching. He has two sons, another N.B. and Chester. He has added cleared fields and is building up his herd by using good registered sires.

Joe took a two-year course at Benhke Walker in Portland and then came back and was graduated from Toutle High School. After he and Alida Mangs were married, they attended Bellingham Normal School. The first year they both went, but the second year their son Rex had made his appearance so only Joe went.

N.B. "Pole" Gardner and his wife, Nellie Gardner. He was the first Toutle storekeeper (1882) and first postmaster (1883). "He fed the hungry."

After they left Bellingham, they came back to Cowlitz County and both taught at Clover Valley for several years. Joe was county superintendent for several years, too. Then, he took a trip to the Washington State Legislature for a term or two.

Joe and family lived on the Nate (Pole) Gardner property. Joe was born December 23, 1892. He died December 10, 1990.

Gardner's Old Toutle Store of 1910

The South Toutle bridge, not far from N.B. Gardner's place. It was built in 1904.

Toutle River District #30. The first school year was 1883. Presumably it was the William Gardner homestead. W.P. Wells taught here in the early 1890s. Joe Gardner (born December 23, 1892) is one of the small children being held up to the window. Family names represented here are Eaton, Gardner, Lapham, Price and Wyant.

A later Toutle School, located near the Nate Gardner home. This building was rendered useless upon the consolidation of Sightly, Silver Lake and Toutle Schools, circa 1930s.

This Green Mountain School was built in 1897 on the Price homestead. A Miss Smith was the first teacher. Lucia Jenkins taught here for a short time. Joe Gardner taught here in the early years of his teaching.

David Gardner, Civil War Vet, Came to Toutle in 1883

by Mrs. Ray Slack, Cowlitz County Advocate, *December 3, 1953:*

Mrs. Alice Robins is the last surviving member of the David Gardner family which came to Toutle in the spring of 1883. She will be 78 years old January 9.

The following information on the Gardner and Gilmore families comes from Mrs. Robins.

David Gardner was born in Illinois in 1840 to Steve and Abigail Gardner. David was the eighth of nine children. His father died when David was quite small. His mother and family moved to Iowa, where David went to school, and from Iowa to Kansas.

David enlisted in the U.S. Army in 1860 and was discharged in 1865 at the end of the Civil War. He met a Miss May Clark and married her. Gardner bought a place in Kansas and lived there until the time when they moved to Washington.

The couple had eight children. Charlie, Eddie and Freddie died in Kansas. Alice, Jessie and Henry were born in Kansas and came to Toutle with their parents. Lillie and Richard were born at Toutle.

Gardner filed on a 160-acre homestead. He lived there for many years and then traded it for another place at Toutle, which was his home until he died.

"In 1883 it was far different than in 1953," Mrs. Robins said. "We have spent many years here, from the ox team to the automobile and airplane age."

Alice Gardner, David's daughter, married John Wallace Gilmore in 1899. Their nine children were William, born in 1900; Grace, 1901; Myrtle, 1903; Robert, 1905; George, 1906; Gerald, 1907; Bertha, 1908; Chester, 1909; and Otis, 1911.

Chester died when a boy. William was killed at work when he was about 36. Mrs. Grace Bermister and Mrs. Myrtle Dyson live in Centralia. Robert, George, Gerald and Otis are at Molalla, Oregon, and Mrs. Bertha Wade is at Independence, Oregon.

John Gilmore died December 13, 1918. Six years later Mrs. Gilmore married Tobias Robins, who died in 1947. Mrs. Gilmore lived with her daughter, Mrs. Bermister, for a while, and then with her son Otis for about two years until his marriage, when he moved to Molalla.

The Frank Smith Story

by Dora Smith Jones

James Franklin Smith was born at Elgin in southeast Kansas on December 14, 1877. He was one year old when his father died, a few months before Frank's brother Clayton was born.

The mother, Lizzie (Evans) Smith brought the brothers to the Northwest about 1889. She presumably traveled with relatives, probably including her three brothers—Charley, Silas and Bosh Evans. Frank was about twelve years old, and he afterwards remembered the Indians riding alongside the train and shooting at the coaches.

Lizzie Smith remarried twice, the second time to a Canadian named Brownell. The children ultimately included, besides the brothers Frank and Clayton, one half-sister (Maudi Price), one half-brother (William Price), and two half-brothers named Brownell.

Frank Smith moved to British Columbia and lived there for a while. He later moved to The Dalles, Oregon, and stayed with his uncle, Silas Evans, before settling in Cowlitz County.

Florence Minnie Black was one of ten children born to Hiram and Clara Black. Florence was born August 11, 1890, at Ceres in Lewis County, Washington.

Frank Smith and Florence Black were married at Doty in 1906. They made their home at Toutle where Frank drove a team of oxen, hauling supplies for Gardner's store. In 1908 they purchased from Len Gardner a 13-acre farm south of the river at the end of a road, which is still known as Frank Smith Road. There were five children—Perry, James, Pearl, Dora and Ray.

Frank, although having a crippled knee, bucked shingle bolts for a livelihood for several years. He then served as the State Forest Ranger in the Toutle District for more than 20 years. That position entitled him to have a telephone, the only one at Toutle at that time. He could talk with other ranger stations and with the lookout on top of Mt. St.

Father, Franklin Smith; Mother, Florence M. Smith; Oldest son, Perry; Second son, James; Oldest daughter, Pearl; Second daughter, Dora; Third son, Ray

Helens. Between fire seasons Frank worked as a logger for Ostrander and Weyerhaeuser.

The family raised beef, hogs and chickens for their own use, and had a big garden each summer, plus fruit from their orchard and wild berries from the logged areas. The children earned spending money in the summer by peeling cascara bark and picking evergreen black-berries, which were collected and sold in Castle Rock.

Attending school at Toutle required a 2-mile hike along a graveled, and some-times muddy, road. A trip to Castle Rock by horse and buggy was a special occasion—for shopping or to attend celebra-tions. The 30-mile round trip invariably took all day. They would always visit at the Jackson Hotel while in Castle Rock, because it was operated by Frank's half-sister, Maude, and her husband, Henry Jackson. The Jacksons had previously homesteaded at a timber claim on Jackson Creek, a tributary of the North Toutle River near Mt. St. Helens.

In 1982 Pearl (Eaton) and Dora (Jones) are still lifetime residents of Cowlitz County. Ray lives in Wrangell, Alaska. The other family members have passed away. (Note: Pearl passed away June 27, 1987.)

Some Settlers Of Toutle & Green Mountain

1879	John Wyant	1884	B.L. Beighle
1881	I.N. Beighle		W.H. Chism
1882	N.B. Gardner	1886	W.A. Berry
	William Gardner		A.J. Orahood
	A.S. Gilmore	1887	J.C. Martin
	L.W. Gilmore	1888	P. McDonald
	L.N. Herring		J.P. Eaton
	Paul Johnson	1889	Jake Tippery
	John Luebke	1890	Charles Erickson
	J.M. Lull	1891	Lester Patchin
	Joseph Price	1894	John Thomas
1883	David Gardner		
	Joseph Hallock		
	Swaine Peterson		

Some Settlers of Green River, North of Toutle River

1890	Victor Carlsen	1891	E.E. Carroll
	S. Johnson		Charles Olsen
	Charlie V. Swanson		W.M. Reisman
	William West	1894	Anton Peterson

Note: Fourteen more settlers were not listed as they may have been in Lewis County.

Kid Valley

by Leland Jackson

Strangers leaving Cowlitz Valley to claim their new homesteads in the Upper Toutle River Valley found the roads from "civilization" to their promised land filled with every conceivable thing that could make the trip difficult and unpleasant.

The first twenty some miles were bad, but after leaving the Gardner's store they were confronted with the biggest obstacle of all. It was known as Green Mountain. There were no bypasses. The wagons must go over the top of it. The route was steep, rough and dangerous.

Some pioneers turned back but most made the arduous trip and came down into a beautiful forested valley that was populated largely by German and Scandinavian people who had preceded them.

It is said that the newcomers, on a closer look, saw children peeking out seemingly from all the nearby trees. The youngsters were the offspring of the large North European families.

Kids, kids, kids, everywhere! Kid Valley was well-named indeed.

Some Settlers of Kid Valley

1888 W.H. Edwards
A.F. Lafferty
1889 T.B. Madden
N.L. Marshall
1890 J.E. Buskirk
Frank Parker

Wm. Henry Chism Had Twelve Children

by Mrs. Ray Slack, from Cowlitz County Advocate, *August 13, 1953:*

Mr. and Mrs. William Henry Chism came from Missouri and landed in Castle Rock March 4, 1889. They moved onto what was known then as the Edwards place, later moving to Kid Valley, where they homesteaded.

Five of the twelve Chism children were born in Missouri and seven here. The five born in Missouri were William, Jr., who died, Bess Price of Castle Rock, Bea Swanson of Chehalis, Minnie Prill of Los Angeles and Stella Iliff of Oakland, California. Those who were born here were Ben, Scott, Frank, Dorothy, who died when she was about twelve years old, Maurice of Tacoma, and Oscar, who lives on Tower Road.

Julia Ellen Chism died in 1927. Her husband, William Henry, died in 1935.

Early-day trip, probably Green Mountain Road (from Lange/Whitney Collection)

Charlie Thomas, early-day trip to the homestead (from Lange/Whitney Collection)

Going my way?
Note puncheon road.

Travel was slow in those days.

Some Settlers of St. Helens Valley

1881 W.S. Grabill
1888 Jake Hamm
        Abraham Umiker
1889 W.S. Covilla
        Mary Sells

1890 Felix Scallen
1891 R.S. Moss
1892 F.S. Scallen

For some reason several homesteaders of upper St. Helen's Valley are not mentioned in the foregoing list. Among those names missing are Cliff Couch and Charles Maratta, in the vicinity of Maratta Creek. Also William Jackson and Henry Jackson, who had claims near Spud Mountain. These four claims were made in the early 1900s. Also, the Lange claim at Spirit Lake is not listed.

PART III

The Railroad, Mills & Shingles

The 1880's

by Leland Jackson

When John Robin moved to the east bank of the Cowlitz River at what is now the foot of Shintaffer Avenue in Castle Rock, no one supposed that this single event was to prove the most important one in the development of Castle Rock and the Toutle Valley.

The same year the Robin's Mill started up, the Northern Pacific Railroad became transcontinental. The Northern Pacific leased the Oregon Railway and Navigation tracks down the south bank of the Columbia to Portland. They then built a track from there to Goble, Oregon. The train ferry *Tacoma* took a complete train to Kalama in one trip. The last trip of this ferry was on Christmas Day, 1908.

Because of the time frame rather than related events, we might put in two items here.

In 1880 there were 24 (this is not a misprint) active road districts in the county. (Since then the number has gradually shrunk to 3 districts—not "road" districts. There is talk of getting rid of all districts as such.)

The winter of 1880-81 was exceptionally cruel and the settlers suffered because of inadequate living quarters. Much livestock perished, and stored food was ruined. Many people were left destitute. Some settlers became discouraged and left their holdings to move elsewhere.

The N.P. was flooding the eastern and central states with literature extolling the virtues of Western Washington. We may imagine that the language used was much like that of Gus Hafenbrack and Long-Bell in the 1920s. Some of the readers will remember those "warm moisture-bearing winds that made for a luxuriant growth," etc. The natives already here call the stuff "rain that made the weeds grow the year around."

When John Robin began operations in 1883, there were men to be hired. The men had to live nearby as there was no ready and rapid transportation from home to work. Houses were needed. Lumber for houses was needed. Single men needed hotels and restaurants. Stores were needed to furnish food and clothing. Almost immediately streets and lots were surveyed. One of the available surveyors was Benjamin F. Ivey. Many of the first houses were of up-and-down construction of rough lumber. There was an almost "instant town" created in that triangular area bounded by Front Street, Cowlitz Avenue and the river.

The Jackson, White, Shintaffer and Conger subdivisions were interspersed by Jackson, Shintaffer, Conger, Cheer and Leaming Streets.

The Kellogg Transportation Co. almost immediately put in a river dock and a sizable warehouse next to Robin's Mill.

The Northern Pacific put in a siding for cars to receive shingles.

In 1885 Robin's shipped the first carload of shingles east of the Rocky Mountains. In recognition of this accomplishment, the railroad paid the tariff to the destination in Pennsylvania.

All these events were in a crowded three years.

Shingles from Silver Lake

John Robin

by Leland Jackson

John Robin is a very important historical figure in the founding and development of early Castle Rock. Up until the present, little was generally known about him other than he built the first shingle mill in Cowlitz County and perhaps in Washington Territory.

The following biographical sketch tells how he happened to land in Monticello in 1859:

Mr. Robin was a son of Thomas de ROBON, a native of Paris, France. Somewhere along his travels, John's name changed to ROBIN.

After arriving in Cowlitz County, he spent four years in the employ of the stage line that made scheduled runs between Monticello and Olympia. He served as a stage driver and as a dispatch rider. In the latter job he carried important mail, papers and money as the occasion demanded.

He married a daughter of Frederick Stock, a native of Berlin, Germany, who had secured a GDLC at Stockport, now known as Pleasant Hill. John was ultimately to father at least two sons. The older, Fred, was born at Monticello, and the younger, Thomas Windsor, later known as Win, was born on the family homestead west of Castle Rock in 1869. This piece of land was later to become the Quick farm.

John and son Fred logged the timber from the land and built a sawmill. (While this mill was in operation, a young man by the name of Arthur Bemus was killed when a shingle saw disintegrated. This is believed to be the first industrial accident in this area.) John later built a shingle mill on the bank of Arkansas Creek (now Delameter Creek) on the claim of Elisha Jackson. This location was ideal in that cedar bolts could be floated down to the mill. The shingles were then stacked on a dock at the mouth of the creek to be picked up by a sternwheeler.

In 1883-84 when the Northern Pacific Railroad was being made transcontinental, John decided to remove and rebuild his mill on the east bank of the Cowlitz River at the west end of what is now Shintaffer Avenue. The east end of Shintaffer was the N.P. station. Shingles could then be shipped either by rail or water.

This mill was the nucleus around which the early village of Castle Rock developed north of Cowlitz Avenue.

In later life, Mr. Robin served in probably every municipal job when he was needed—mayor, councilman, municipal judge, or fire chief. There is no record of his ever working as city marshall, however.

Shingles

by Leland Jackson

Ten years after John Robin shipped his first shingles to eastern United States, the *Cowlitz County Advocate* reported: "The output of shingles for Cowlitz County for the year 1895 is about 107,000,000, and of these about 75,000,000 have been manufactured in and tributary to Castle Rock."

Obviously, Robin's Mill had much help in such production. In the course of a few years, such names as Metcalf Shingle Company, Peabody, Byerly, Barnes and Bull, Caswell and Daub, Bemis Brothers, Dean Swift, Malone, Sturm, Dickson, and many others were shipping shingles by water and rail.

Before these mills could operate they had to have the red cedar logs or bolts ready for the chutes. For ease of handling, most trees were cut into bolts. These bolts were usually 56 inches long and split into a size that two men could readily load on sleds or wagons. The bolts were paid for by the cord. A cord was a stack 8 feet long and 4 feet high. As time went on, the bolt size became more or less standardized. Then, by rule of thumb, 18 were assumed to constitute a cord. In actual practice, money changed hands on the number of bolts delivered at the mill. Some timber owners cut their own bolts and delivered them to the mill or river bank. In other cases, the timber was bought and "bolt camps" were set up. Some of these camps were quite large, and the families moved out in the forests to be with and to furnish homes for the men.

In 1903-04 my mother, Melle Lee Jackson, taught school at a camp on Leyton's Prairie in Lewis County. The bolts were floated down the Cowlitz River from there.

Horse-drawn sleds on greased skid roads were the usual method of getting the bolts to the river. All bolts were stamped on each end with a registered, impressed brand to show the ownership.

River drivers could be characterized as a nearly separate breed of being. Some men followed this work almost exclusively. Axes, saws, peaveys, and pike poles, along with a special type of double-ended row-boats, were the tools of the trade. When all was ready for the "drive" and there was sufficient water in the stream, the bolts were dumped in.

The drivers had no hope of staying dry, but they could keep warm by wearing heavy wool clothing. The heavy "cork" shoes, although they might be new, were punctured to allow the water to drain out.

When the day was done, the crew would take their bedding out of the boat and eat the meal made ready by the cook who had gone ahead. The men usually slept under a tree and the bedding was not always dry. Many times a drive would last a month or more.

When the drive was nearing its destination, the mill crew would stretch a boom across the river to shear the bolts into the proper pocket boom.

An endless link belt chain, revolving in a chute, powered by a steam engine, was then used to pile the bolts on the bank. One end of the chute was in the river. This elevator also was used to put the bolts back in the water when the mill was ready to use them.

In the course of many years, several machines were developed to saw and trim the shingles. First, there was a *hand machine*. Then came the *single block*, and then the *double block*. All these machines required a *knot sawyer* or *clipper*. These men trimmed the raw edges and cut out the knots.

Finally, there was a machine developed that was known as the *up-right*. This machine had two saws at right angles to each other. One sawed the shingles from a powered carriage. The other one was the clipper. The operator of this machine, known as the *sawyer*, took the shingles from one saw and trimmed them on another. In the course of time, all the other systems were discarded.

Some experimental machines were not successful. The *Chaloner Ten Block* was set up in at least one local mill. This machine had carriages for ten blocks around the circumference of a large wheel. Two saws were set up to cut a shingle as each block passed by. This machine was used for some time but could operate efficiently with but two blocks instead of ten.

Probably the most unconventional shingle machine was set up on the bank of the Cowlitz at the mouth of the Arkansas Creek. There were no saws on this machine. The blocks were steamed until they were soft, and the carriage forced the blocks past sharp blades. A shingle was shaved off each time a block passed by. It made beautiful shingles, but as soon as they dried out on the roof they curled up and cracked. According to my father, Parde Jackson, who worked on this machine, known locally as *the sausage grinder*, it fell into the river during the 1906 flood, never to be retrieved. It had been abandoned for some time prior to its drowning. Some obscure notes indicate that the above machine was imported and set up by a Mr. Sturm.

Shingle saws took a high toll of fingers, especially the *knot saw*. Strangers visiting Castle Rock would remark about the number of men with missing fingers.

Cedar Drives On Toutle Required Tough Men

Mrs. Jessie Wilt, Special Writer, The Daily News, *Saturday & Sunday, June 21-22, 1970*

To look at the Toutle River today, it is hard to imagine it filled from bank to bank with a drive of cedar. (A drive was a consignment of logs or shingle bolts that the rivermen took charge of to deliver downstream where needed.) But, beginning in the 1870s and continuing until the early 1920s, the drives were a regular event.

The trees were felled by hand with a crosscut saw sometimes known as a *misery whip*. Then, they were cut into 4' 4" lengths and split into 4 pieces. These pieces, known as *bolts*, were placed on sleds made of vine maple and hauled to the river bank with oxen or horses. Here they were stockpiled until October or November when the fall rains would raise the river level.

Driving crews were sent out by the mills at Castle Rock and Kelso and usually consisted of seven or eight men, plus a cook. They were accompanied by a cook boat and a blanket boat. They were paid $3 a day and worked from daylight until dark. The boat pullers got two-bits a day extra.

A sudden drop in the river level would leave thousands of bolts high and dry on the gravel bars. Then, they had to be manhandled back into the water. When dry, they were heavy, but after a few days in the river, they were something else.

Max Feist, one of the few old-timers left who worked on the

drives, still lives at Toutle. He started on the river in 1906 when he was seventeen. He smiles now as he describes riding the bolts in fast water on a frosty morning—"Riding was fun but a misstep meant a dunking in the cold water, and the rest of the day spent in wet clothes. There was no time to stop and change, and no dry clothes handy anyway. It took 16 days from Kid Valley to Castle Rock, and you wore out a pair of "cork" shoes on one drive because of the rocks. There was often ice on the water, and if the grub boat swamped, things got even more uncomfortable."

Fred Mangs, still living on the farm at Toutle where he was born, started on the river when he was 14 years old. Foreman of a driving crew before he turned 21, he drove for both the Peabody Mill and the Robin Mill at Castle Rock. Now 73 years old, he says it was hard work but enjoyable, and he'd like to make another drive. And, he is alert and agile enough to do it, too.

Joe Gardner also remembers the drives, although he was only a small boy at the time. He tells how he and his brother would catch a bolt and ride it down the river to where a jam had built up, climb off, and go back upriver to catch another ride. This nearly ended in disaster when his brother didn't get off quickly enough and was sucked under the jam. Joe says he ran crying down the river, certain his brother was done for. Then, in a small area of clear water below the hangup, his brother popped to the surface—soaked, scared, but unhurt.

This particular jam finally piled up 4,000 cords of cedar in one massive blockade. The drivers fought for many days trying to get the wood floating again. They had to make a small opening in the face of the jam and gradually guide the cedar through, being careful not to open the face too wide or they would lose the backwater and leave all the cedar high and dry.

There were also cedar drives on other rivers in this area, and these sometimes utilized a splash dam to back up enough water to float the cedar downstream.

Cedar was an important source of income and brought the only "cash money" into the area. Stores and banks extended credit against this crop. The market was good and the price was stable. Nearly everyone had an interest, one way or another, in the drives.

That is why the big flood in the 1890s created such havoc. Several drives were already under way and a large stock of bolts was in the booms along the Cowlitz. Then, the rains started and forgot to stop. The rivers raised higher and higher, and still it rained. Piles of bolts on the side streams were washed into the rivers. These all came tearing down on the flood to hit the booms in the main river, and everything washed out to sea. When the waters receded, the streams were stripped of cedar, and the people had nothing to show for the year's hard labor.

Many spent the rest of their lives paying off the effects of this loss. (Read of N.B. Gardner's loss in this flood.)

Many tales are told of the drivers. George Studebaker was the only person to ever put the camp boat through Hollywood Gorge without being roped down. Jake Tippery drove the river for the most years. The last drive was taken down by Seth Tippery and Billy Sutton, from Jordan Creek on the South Toutle to Castle Rock. Fred Mangs was on one drive when the going was so poor it took 30 days from Soda Springs to the Toutle River. The Anderson brothers—Charlie, Oscar, Fred and Ted—worked on the North Toutle close to the Skamania County line. They had one drive that only took six days to Castle Rock, with perfect water all the way.

The men who drove logs on the river were known as *River Rats*, but the cedar bolt drivers were called *Slough Boars*. One old driver said that after two weeks on the river the reason for this was obvious from 40 feet downwind.

But, the story that best illustrates the hardiness of these men concerns an especially rough stretch of water where the cook boat was capsized. The foreman yelled, "Save the bacon, boys!" But, the crew yelled, "To hell with the bacon! Save the whiskey!"

The Advocate, June 10, 1897: "Bemis' Shingle Mill which has been delayed in starting up on account of the jam of bolts in the Toutle River, will be put in operation this week. Wm. Studebaker made a drive of 150,000 feet of logs from his camp above Castle Rock Monday last. We are informed that the logs will be rafted at Kelso."

The Advocate, November 26, 1897: "Although the Cowlitz lacked three feet of reaching the high water mark of November 1896, it was high enough to take out a thousand or more cord of shingle bolts to the big boom at the mouth of the river. Several families living on the lower grounds of this city were forced to room on higher land for two or three days. Most of the bolts going out came from the Toutle boom, where the big loss came from last year. Of the bolts that went into the big boom, 100 cord belonged to W.A. Wright and 900 cord to Abe Umiker and other citizens of Toutle. The 900 cord was intended for the Duniway Mill operated by O.J. Brown. The Wright bolts were for the Bemis Mill, which also lost its shear boom Friday." (*Cowlitz County Historical Society Quarterly*)

Gilligohike

Bolts on a wagon

PART IV

The Mt. St. Helens Area

Historical Data

Assembled by Bea Buzzetti, January 18, 1951

In geologic development, the Cascade Region was uplifted and then worn back to a comparative level, perhaps many times. Bailey Willis, Professor of Geology at Stanford University in 1881, has conclusively proved that this has happened at least once before the last uplift, which came in recent geologic time. This last huge upheaval caused by internal stress took a north-to-south trend, extending about 300 miles (from Mt. Baker to Lassen Peak) with a width of about 50 miles. During continual upheaval, huge blocks tilted at various angles, and in some places, changed by heat and pressure, uplifted with forces of volcanism.

The crest line is fairly even, 5000 to 8000 feet in elevation. Above this rise volcanic peaks of a later date—Pleistocene, about two million years ago—the results of molten lava escaping through fractures made at the time the mountain blocks were lifted. And, because the lava was cooler and the openings less extensive, the force became more explosive, heaping up material in cones along lines of fracture. The peaks take on a north-to-south trend, as does the main range, and include Baker, Glacier, Rainier, Adams, St. Helens, Hood, Jefferson, Three Sisters, and others.

Mt. St. Helens—youngest of the peaks (altitude 9671 feet) and sometimes called the "Fujiyama of the West" because of its symmetrical form—was discovered May 19, 1792, by Captain George Vancouver. On October 20 of that same year, he gave it the name of Mt. St. Helens in honor of his Britannic Majesty's ambassador at the court of Madrid.

One eruption of Mt. St. Helens occurred on November 22, 1842, throwing ashes as far as the Dalles, 60 miles distant. The eruption poured forth, on the south side, somewhere near Butte camp, elevation of 4,500 feet, cascading and flowing down a number of old valleys for nearly ten miles to the Lewis River. An old French Canadian voyager said of this volcano, "The light from the burning volcano at my cabin 20 miles away was so intense that one could see to pick up a pin in the grass at midnight."

About 6 miles southeast of the base of the mountain, a most unusual lava cave was discovered in 1895 by Olie Peterson while hunting deer. It has been identified as the one referred to by Fremont as being active on November 22, 1842. The lava, cooling first on the outside, has left a lava tunnel, said to be one and a half miles long (one of the largest of its kind in North America), winding up toward the mountain like a river. Air currents flow through this cave, making it safe for travel, and it has been explored for almost a mile. The grade is about 3%, the bed 20 feet wide with banks 6 feet high. The roof of the cave, a 20-foot arch, averages 15 feet below the surface of the ground. The cave is of glazed brown lava decorated with tiny stalactites. It can be entered one and a half miles beyond the wagon road on the north fork of the Lewis River. Geologists from Yale University have done some research work in this area.

Recent activity is also evidenced by the lava tree wells to the south and west of the mountain. Here lava surrounded the standing trees, making a natural kiln with such intense heat that the wood was sometimes reduced to pure charcoal. An article written in 1917 by Alida Bigelow, a Seattle Mountaineer, states, "To the north and west along the west top of the Boot, steam caves and flumaroles give evidence of the internal heat of the peak." Joe Hazard, in his book *Snow Sentinels of the Pacific*, states that during a climb on May 30, 1926, he noted hot spots on the "Lizard" where the heat of the cone breaks through. H.F. Samuelsen of the Forest Service made this statement, "About 1928 I saw some steam coming out of a bare spot on the south side about 1000 feet down from the summit."

From 1802 to 1836 is the estimated date of the next most recent lava flow on Mt. St. Helens. Dr. Donald B. Lawrence of the University of Minnesota, who has made an extensive study of this region, states that evidence shows that this lava flow slowly poured forth from beneath the center of the Toutle glacier carrying on its upper surface glacial silt. This perhaps occurred in the wet season since the heat radiated from it did not start a forest fire. However, vegetation was killed for a distance of 40 feet on the steep side. Borderline trees which, though injured, survived the intense heat, live today, their scars revealing the history of this event.

Dr. Lawrence suggests 1802 as the approximate date of the largest pumice deposit, covering the area north of Mt. St. Helens. That many of the old trees living on the south shore of Spirit Lake lived through this eruption is evidenced by the pumice piled up on top of their uppermost roots. Examination of wood cores shows a series of very narrow rings starting about 1802 and increasing in size with each year, becoming normal after about ten years. The pumice (a hardened volcanic glass froth, the cavities of which are produced by the expulsion of water vapor at a high temperature as lava comes to the surface) is gray in color. Explosions within the crater blew this molten froth high into the air where it cooled quickly and settled on the surrounding country. St. Helens pumice has been found as far as 20 miles to the northwest. It is so light and porous that it has given this area the name of being the place where rocks float. Try it sometime. Throw a dry pebble into the water and frequently it will float like a piece of wood.

Pumice eruptions at an earlier date, perhaps 100 years or more before that time, covered tree trunks in the Spirit Lake area with hot pumice to a depth of from 12 to 20 feet. These trunks, somehow shut off from air so that they could not continue burning, remained in place. Ground waters brought in fine sand, and the entire area packed solid. Later, the trees rotted out, leaving their casts. The Spirit Lake area has quite a number of these natural tree wells scattered through the forest. They present a hazard to those who wander off the beaten trails.

Beautiful Spirit Lake (elevation 3199 feet) is set in a huge amphitheater facing Mt. St. Helens. It occupies what was once a forested valley; the steep timbered walls now rise about 2000 feet above the lake. The greatest measured depth (or height) of the trunk of an ancient forest giant, which barely protrudes above the water, was 120 feet. Perhaps the primary cause of the damming of the Toutle River to form the lake was the glacial outwash. Coe's Dam, at the outlet of Spirit Lake, was built after 1900, but it raised the level only one or two feet. The lake covers 1800 acres and is approximately two and a half miles long.

As one leaves Spirit Lake and approaches the mountain through pine and fir forest, the soil is practically all pumice, with little wash from the valley sides. On approaching timberline, altitude 4500 feet, firs disappear, giving way to a forest characteristic of low and middle altitudes of the Pacific Northwest, mostly lodgepole pines and white pines. The newness of the mountain is depicted in this low timberline and the scarcity of vegetation on its slopes. Unlike other peaks, almost no alpine meadows are found above timberline, and heather slopes are absent. The mountain is too new for flower gardens, and the slopes to snow line are bare pumice except for the wild strawberry vines which produce a most delicately flavored berry. Cinders, ash, pumice, and lava cover the slopes on all sides of the mountain. Long swathes are cut through the forest by lava flows too recent for vegetation.

The first ascent of Mt. St. Helens was made by a party headed by Thomas J. Dryer, founder of *The Oregonian*, in 1853. Since that time, thousands of people have enjoyed the gorgeous view from her heights. There are several possible routes requiring an average of 7 hours for the ascent.

During the first years of the 20th Century, there was much mining activity in this vicinity. In 1901 County Commissioner Studebaker built the road from Castle Rock to Spirit Lake to gratify the demands of prospectors. Many claims were staked and thousands expended. Some copper was removed from the St. Helens lode, but a paying lode was never

Mt. St. Helens and Spirit Lake, Wash. (from a postcard in 1906)

located. 1906 marks the date of the first telephone line from Lange to Castle Rock. Mt. Margaret, rising above Spirit Lake on the north, was named for Maggie Layton of Toledo by A. Hofer, a prospector before 1900. In 1913 the rangers' headquarters was moved from the Toutle to Spirit Lake and a lookout station built on Mt. St. Helens. The lookout station has since been removed.

Afterword

by Leland Jackson

For those of us living along the Cowlitz River on May 18, 1980, the full impact of startling, but incomplete, news of the eruption of Mt. St. Helen was a bit slow in developing. A full spectrum of rumors did perhaps instill a feeling of insecurity that varied with individuals, but there was no general anxiety, fear or panic.

Little did we realize what had happened—and was happening. Many of us walked down to the river dike awaiting what we assumed would be a surge of water from the Toutle River—not unlike the flash floods we had seen before.

The deluge never arrived until after dark, and when it did, the flood came to within 15 inches of the top of the dike. The north end of town was evacuated.

The flood tide stood at this point for several hours. The narrow channel at Hollywood Gorge (on the Toutle River) had restricted the flow that otherwise would have flooded the town. The next morning a sulfurous, acrid vapor arose from a flowing river of a mixture of pumice, wood trash, and some water that had a consistency of gravy, and a temperature that killed the trees along the shoreline.

We shook our heads in disbelief. Something had happened, but we were still not sure what it was.

Fifteen years later we are still shaking our heads trying to get a picture of what really happened.